FREEDOM, GRACE, DESTINY

FREEDOM, GRACE, *and* DESTINY

An Interpretation of Existence

Romano Guardini

Translated from the German
FREIHEIT, GNADE, SCHICKSAL
by John Murray, S.J.

CLUNY
Providence, Rhode Island

CLUNY EDITION, 2023

This Cluny edition is a republication of the 1961
Pantheon Books edition of *Freedom, Grace, and Destiny.*

For more information regarding this title
or any other Cluny Media publication,
please write to info@clunymedia.com, or to
Cluny Media, P.O. Box 1664, Providence, RI 02901

VISIT US ONLINE AT WWW.CLUNYMEDIA.COM

ISBN: 978-1685952259

IMPRIMI POTEST: John Coventry, S.J., *Praep. Prov. Angl. Soc. Jesu*
LONDON, AUGUST 4, 1960

NIHIL OBSTAT: James T. Clarke, S.T.L., *Censor Librorum*

IMPRIMATUR: Jerome D. Hannan, D.D., *Bishop of Scranton*
SCRANTON, DECEMBER 20, 1960

The Nihil obstat *and* Imprimatur *are official declarations that a book or pamphlet is considered to be free of doctrinal or moral error. No implication is contained therein that those who have granted them agree with the contents, opinions, or statements expressed.*

Cover design by Clarke & Clarke
Cover image: Giovanni Battista da Faenza, *The Incredulity of Saint Thomas* (detail), c. 1500–1515, oil on panel
Courtesy of Wikimedia Commons

CONTENTS

INTRODUCTION (1)

Freedom (5)

FREEDOM AS FORM OF ACTION (6)
The Nature of Free Behaviour—The Forms of Free Activity—Free Activity as Task

FREEDOM AND THE CONTENT OF ACTION (18)
Freedom in Act and Freedom in Content—Freedom in Immediate Sentiment, in Experience of Nature, in Relation to Things and to One's Own Body—Freedom in the Realization of Values—Freedom in Personal Relationship—Moral Freedom—Freedom in Religion—Résumé—The Subject of Freedom

CHRISTIAN FREEDOM (52)
St. Paul's Experience of Grace—Act and Content of Christian Freedom—The Eschatological Mark of Christian Freedom—The Relation of Christian to Natural Freedom—Appendix: The Logical Problem of the Free Act

Grace (83)

THE "GRACIOUS" AS AN ELEMENT OF IMMEDIATE EXISTENCE (85)
The "Gracious" in Relation to Authority—The Creative: Inspiration and Achievement—Encounter and Union—Euphoria and the Perfect—The Grace Element in Being—Grace in the Religious Sphere

GRACE IN THE CHRISTIAN SENSE (101)
The Creation of the World and Grace—Grace in Christian Existence—The Relation of Grace, Properly So Called, to "Graciousness" as an Element in the World—Excursus: Work

Destiny (131)

THE ELEMENTS OF OUR EXPERIENCE OF DESTINY (132)
Necessity—The Fact—Chance—Destiny in Man Himself

THE RELIGIOUS AND THE PERSONAL ELEMENTS IN THE EXPERIENCE OF DESTINY (147)
The Religious Character of Destiny—The Subject of This Experience of Destiny

THE CONQUEST OF DESTINY (153)
The Support of Destiny, Struggle with Destiny, and the Influence of Its Source—Fatalism, Stoicism, and Humour—Destiny as Task

DESTINY AND REVELATION (163)
The Transformation of This Experience of Destiny in Faith—Destiny in the Life of Jesus—Destiny and Providence—Destiny and Judgment—Providence and the Values of Destiny—Excursus: The Element of Tragedy

Introduction

THE studies contained in this volume are inspired by the same principle that inspired the works collected in *Welt und Person* (1940), *Unterscheidung des Christlichen* (1935), and *Auf dem Wege* (1923) and which has provided a basic directive for all my work, namely, the attempt to view the pattern of Christian existence as a whole.

Early Christian thought had this universal view. Augustine draws no methodological division between philosophy and theology or, in philosophy, between metaphysics and psychology, within theology, between theoretical dogma and practical application to life but his mind proceeds from the whole of Christian existence to consider the total pattern and its different parts. The position remained fundamentally the same till the peak point of the Middle Ages had been passed. Thomas Aquinas took considerable trouble to draw critical distinctions as well as to give a comprehensive synthesis. But the basis of his thinking was, none the less, the living consciousness of the unity of Christian existence, as world and grace.

Then the division sets in. Philosophy is separated from theology, empirical science from philosophy, practical instruction from knowledge of reality. The effort was not unjustified and has resulted in numerous valuable consequences, but it has its perilous side because it deepens and solidifies the disintegration of modern man.

I shall not pursue this topic further; it would demand an analysis of
2 the whole cultural situation in which we are placed. I am concerned with the fact that the conscious unity of existence has been to a large extent lost even by believing Christians. The believer no longer stands with his faith amid the concrete, actual world, and he no longer rediscovers that world in his faith. He has made a grim necessity of this dismemberment by constructing, if we may employ the term, a chemically pure faith in which he insists upon seeing the true form of orthodoxy. This orthodoxy has a somewhat austere and very courageous quality, but we must not forget that it is an emergency position. To save redemption by the Son it has been forced to abandon creation by the Father. Yet the sentence "He who sees me, sees the Father" (John 14:9) has logically as its reverse the further sentence, "Who will not see the Father, does not see me any more." This basic situation has given rise to different kinds of Christian existence. Faith has perhaps taken refuge in inwardness and left the world to its own devices; or all that we understand by grace receives a purely negative relation to the world and the result is a paradox—something that cannot possibly exist and yet has to be postulated; or it may attempt to justify a worldly, scientific outlook through a new apologetic that seeks to build its bridges—a true work of Sisyphus—without asking whether the chasms exist that they are meant to cross. Or, finally, if it has not already succumbed to these difficulties, it makes its peace with the new secularism and becomes a mere religious philosophy and ethic.

I am not implying that faith in itself has grown more feeble. This has been frequently suggested but, in my opinion, quite unjustly. The man of our age who does believe has often a more conscious and courageous and—it might be added—a more heroic faith than was so in earlier periods. The final judgment will one day reveal how frequently and how completely the New Testament description of faith as the "victory that overcometh the world" (1 John 5:4) will have been realized in these our times. Yet this faith has increasingly lost contact with the world and grown increasingly incapable of grasping and fashioning it: in theory, as a complete *Weltanschauung* or world outlook, a vision and understanding of the world from the standpoint of faith; in the practical sphere, as a true method, based upon reality and truth, of saving the objects and values of our human life that are threatened with continual perils. From this same source derive in large measure the triviality and emptiness which affect religious thought and activity at many a point. The riches of revelation are inexhaustible, but we have to put our questions to them, and these questions come from the reality of the world. Equally unbounded are the possibilities for action which lie in the figure and power of Christ, but they have to be discovered, and we discover them in the measure in which real life approaches Christ.

The time has come for us to take our stand again, to think and live, in Christian existence as a whole, in the sense of the Pauline words: "All is yours but you are Christ's" (1 Cor. 3:23). It is time to realize that all divisions have only a methodological value and that what really exists is the world and man in the world, as called by God and judged and redeemed. It is time for us to consider the whole as a whole. In the process we shall preserve all that has been won in the long, sustained efforts of previous centuries: a critical conscience, careful differentiation, and the serious discussion of scientific questions. Our formula is in no sense one of "back to the past," whether to the Middle Ages or the early Christian period. It can only be a forward movement, transcending divisions to attain to the whole, with the approach which once was that of Western man but which now, after an interval of five hundred years, has become more critical, more earnest, and more detached.

As far as reflection is concerned, we must study a phenomenon not merely as it appears by itself but as it runs through all the dimensions—depth, breadth, and height—of existence understood in the Christian sense, and we must endeavour to grasp its significance from the combined standpoints of psychology, philosophy, and theology, in such a way, however, that we incur no charge of crossing frontiers unduly or confusing the territories in which we work. It is evident that this claim has a number of latent dangers which belong to the spoken word in all its forms, particularly in education, propaganda, and communication. In fairness it may be stated that these are no mere negative attitudes but positive expressions of our disintegrated existence and of its craving for eventual unity.

This Introduction might be criticized from several points of view, not least on the ground that it is unwise to provide a yardstick by which the book that it introduces may be measured. But, when I assure the reader that it makes no claim to measure up to this yardstick, I remain modestly within the dimensions of my earlier work, which I have never regarded as anything but a search that was continually renewed. I trust that this volume too will be understood and accepted in that spirit.

Freedom

THE PROBLEM

Our inquiry begins with the problem of freedom. And it does so by going back to immediate experience and asking: What is my manner of life? Do all the acts which I perform arise in the same way or can fundamental differences be detected in them? Can I discover in the total pattern one kind of behaviour that stands out from the rest and compels me to apply a special name to it—a name which continually recurs when men discuss themselves, the name of freedom?

As soon as this phenomenon has been clearly brought out, we can formulate the further question: In what does the essence of this behaviour consist, and what is its significance in the whole pattern of existence?

ROMANO GUARDINI

6 FREEDOM AS FORM OF ACTION

The Nature of Free Behaviour

I know by experience that I am alive. Interior impulses and external influences elicit from me the most diversified responses. But, quite apart from their subject, these reveal a fundamental distinction. Many of them—for example, the functioning of organs, involuntary reactions to helpful or harmful events, compulsion in its various forms, whatever comes under the heading of habit—take place necessarily. In these it is not really "myself" that is the agent but a "something" in and around myself: my psychophysical system, my natural and social environment, the historical situation—whatever comes into play without co-operation on my part. Consequently, these activities "belong" to me only in a restricted sense. Certainly I have to suffer their consequences, since they occur within my sphere of existence and life, but I neither can nor indeed wish to identify myself with them in that ultimate sense which establishes genuine origin.

But I discover in myself other activities in which I am "myself" really and properly the agent. And here I am conscious of myself as the effective starting point of the process, which must now be more precisely termed the action. It begins in me: not only in the sense in which a mechanical movement derives from the engine of a machine or a plant develops from a seed or a feeling from an interior tension. These are merely instances of a transformation of external forces or the unfolding of an organic potentiality or the emergence of a psychological mood. The acts referred to above involve on the other hand a genuine beginning. Naturally, the act in question supposes certain material prerequisites such as energy, materials, objects, and instruments; but in itself it proceeds from a real starting point, from an interior and *original* source. It happens because

I want it to happen, because I bring it *originally* out of myself; I am the *original* power that lifts it above the threshold of existence.

Consequently, free activity belongs to me in a special manner and, in so far as I perform it, I am in a particular way myself. In addition to passing through me it has emerged from me. It has not only grown out of me, it really and properly began in me so that I was responsible for its inception. I was not only the *original ground* but also the *original active force* in its production.[1] I was not an efficient "something," which as such would presuppose other preceding "things," but a *self*, a subsistent, self-conscious, and effective person.[2] In free activity the action is mine in a unique way and in it I am genuinely myself. Free activity is the essential form of my self-expression, the expression of my personal existence.

Here, to forestall future discussions, it must be insisted that this self capable of freedom is a real self. Critical philosophy distinguishes between the sphere of real being on the one side which has the character of Nature, has therefore nothing to do with freedom, and operates exclusively according to a pattern of necessity and, on the other side, the realm of freedom, postulated by ethical principles but remaining unreal to our intelligence. As a concrete being, man is part of Nature, is a mere biophysical individual in the same category as the crystal, the plant, and the animal. He is a self, a free person, only in the non-real realm of regulative and affective principles. But this interpretation avoids the central problem which is that of the relation of the real self with its

---

1. Translator's Note: The German text has a play on the prefix *Ur* which it is not possible to reproduce in English. The act is said to proceed from an *Ur-sprung*, an original source because I lift it out of myself (*weil ich sie aus mir heraushebe*), and I am therefore its *Ur-heber* (the person who originally lifts it into existence). I was not merely the *Ur-sache*, the original ground from which it came, but also the *Ur-heber*, the primal active agent.
2. For a discussion of the limits of this immanent power and initiative, that is, of the relation between finite and absolute personality, cf. pp. 49, 56ff.

real freedom in the real world. For in addition to the material substrate of chemicophysical matter, in the inanimate sphere, and the impersonal basis of biological existence with plants and animals the world includes the free person capable of action.

The self is active in free behaviour; but it is not this behaviour which brings it into being, nor does it consist only in this. The "Actualist" philosophy interprets this in the sense that the person exists only at the moment of free activity. But this would leave us with an activity without substantial basis within which the self would suddenly emerge—the same monstrous idea, on a limited scale, as that of the absolute spirit realizing itself on an unlimited scale in the world process. What comes first is not action but existence, in this case the existent person. From this the action proceeds. Freedom is found, in the first place, in the personal, that is, the responsible, human being.[3] Free behaviour is the way in which the person actualizes his being with its orientation towards freedom.

The Forms of Free Activity

Free activity has its own particular structure. To start with, you have a self-contained unity of the person. As the activity develops, this unity disintegrates. There is a moment of initiative that detaches itself from the surrounding circumstances as from its own being and capacity; it examines the given possibilities and decides in favour of one among them; it then commits itself to this and thereby realizes itself; when the activity is complete, it re-establishes its unity, enriched now by the tension it has experienced and still more with a new significant content.

This operation may take place in different ways. In one form, that moment of initiative seeks to raise itself "above" the actual situation and itself, to transcend the different elements such as impulses, aptitudes,

3. Cf. Guardini, *Welt und Person* (1940), pp. 83ff.

interests, and inclinations, and to arrive at an independent survey and assessment. This experience of freedom is always present to some degree but it is especially developed in men with high qualities of intelligence and will power, the experience of "choice." Its extreme instance is the completely independent "indifferent" disposition of self and external circumstances, regardless of all other considerations. Creative or highly sensitive persons enjoy another kind of liberty experienced as follows. The moment of initiative seeks to penetrate through superficial layers into the interior reality of the situation and the living self in order to discover and realize the most harmonious result. Its tendency is to discover the inner essence and express this in activity. Its extreme instance is the feeling that "I can't act otherwise. Here I am most fully myself." This attitude of mind should not be confused with compulsion through pressure or habit. It too is based upon that detachment from self and the realization of one possibility among others of which we have been speaking, but the whole movement in this case is "inwards" and not, as in the other, "upwards."[4]

These two forms of free action can never be entirely separated. Now one, now the other is prominent according to the temperament of the agent; but every now and then the opposite form must be also present. Were it not anchored in an expression of the real essence the choice might lose contact with reality and become arbitrary; without the flexibility of choice self-expression might become imprisoned in the strait jacket of being. These two forms of action are the poles of a living pattern which, as always in concrete fact, receives a particular emphasis from one or the other side.[5]

---

4. This contrast may help us to determine the ordinary distinction in the freedom structure of man and woman. For "upwards" and "inwards" as the fundamental directives of Guardini's sphere of existence, cf. *Welt und Person*, pp. 28ff.
5. Cf. Guardini, *Versuch einer Philosophie des Lebendig-Konkreten* (1925), pp. 209ff.

Thus my experience of myself reveals one kind of attitude that is
10 clearly differentiated from other attitudes, and to it by common consent the particular name of freedom is given. It is so out of the ordinary as to disturb the critical philosophers. So many weighty arguments can be brought against the trustworthiness of the experience on which it is based that one may lose one's sense of what is possible and likely. But no sooner has the poor bewildered person retired from the hurly-burly of discussion and turned back to himself than he knows that it is none the less the truth. In spite of everything I am free. Of course my attitude is not always that of a free person; frequently, not at all, in other instances, only partially, but in many a case it is evidently and completely so. When I perform this act, I am aware that my action really proceeds from myself, that I am responsible for it, that I could act differently and, if so, for the sole reason that I wish to. I recognize in myself an element capable of setting an event in motion without myself being set in motion from any other source whatsoever: "initiative," initial energy, the power to bring into being.[6]

The existence of this genuine potentiality and this power of initiating events is proved by two special symptoms of which we are continually conscious: the sense of duty and the sense of responsibility. The former will be considered subsequently. Here we shall speak only of the latter, that characteristic awareness that speaks as follows: My share in what I have done is not merely more extensive; it is fundamentally different. I have to shoulder the consequences of my activity as in everything I do. But I must also accept responsibility for the fact that it has occurred at all. I answer for its good and harmful results, not merely exteriorly and juridically but inwardly with the very kernel of my being. The

6. For the logical problems connected with freedom, cf. Appendix at end of chapter, pp. 75ff.

significance and force of the action are referred back to me. More precisely, the act shows that this intention was in me already and it helped to establish the act. The act sets me under a special standard of judgment to be studied later in greater detail, that of the Good and Right, and it gives significance to myself.

This does not mean, as Psychologism asserts, any hypostatization of a psychological structure as though certain attitudes, essential for the permanence of personality, were projected beyond personality and received an absolute binding force. Nor does it refer, as some sociologists claim, to the interplay of social interests which makes a man accept a habit that restricts his individual inclinations. It is much more a question of some primal element which can be noted in germ at the simplest levels of consciousness, both social and individual. The contrary is true. Man's life is subject to ultimate and supra-personal obligations and it flourishes only when it obeys them, just as the community is right in imposing certain claims upon the individual, not because it desires to be self-assertive but because the claims are in themselves valid.

The sentence, "I am responsible," is rich with meaning. It signifies that I am asked and must answer—more exactly, must justify myself, answer in such a manner that I come into the answer and am caught up in it. And so the very reality we were considering earlier is now revealed from another angle. What provides the object of the question? Not, essentially, the event itself nor its preconditions but rather, who did it, who acted; and further, from what motives, with what intention, and in what frame of mind did he act? This question could never be put to an inanimate thing and not properly to a plant or animal, in other words, not to a "thing" at all. It makes sense only when the reply can come in terms of "I." And where does it come from? Who can put it? Again, not a thing, for a thing can ask no question; nor can existence as a whole, nor a principle or an idea. These have validity but no initiative. They lack a "countenance," the ability to turn around and address a man. Besides, the principle is part of the question because it is the only source of the Right. In consequence, the question to which a personal answer must be given can be asked only by another Person, whose reality is identical with the principle itself, namely, God. Responsibility is directed essentially towards God. Thus it is made clear, as we shall discuss later, that man's freedom is fundamentally a freedom before God.

Free Activity as Task

The act and the attitude of freedom are not self-evident. To begin with, liberty has limits. Action very frequently proceeds not from choice but from necessity or habit. Very often it emerges not from fundamental but from superficial and therefore more insistent levels of our being such as impulses, instincts of preservation and adaptation. But even within its proper boundaries liberty is not only strenuous and fraught with serious consequences, it is burdened with the feeling of responsibility. Accordingly it must be deliberately willed.

The attitude of freedom does not spring from organs secure in their functioning, it is an actualization of personal being, but this need not always follow. It is both astonishing and disturbing to what extent men can abandon a free existence, withdraw themselves, for instance, from its requirements and live in a mere whirl of biological, psychological, and social instincts, and this on a highly cultivated as well as a crude and gross level: both in primitive conditions, in which the individual is still entirely embedded in the life of the community so that everything is carried out according to inviolable rules, and even in mature civilizations, where a long tradition has produced a rich formal world with appropriate modes of behaviour for every conceivable situation. These forms have become a "Nature" in a higher sense, so that everything takes place, as it were, automatically, and little room is left for freedom. The first is an example of a freedom that has not yet awakened, the second of a freedom that, after long and earnest efforts in free activity, has gone to sleep.

But man can also be weaned from the exercise of freedom. Those whose personal formation had its roots in the years before the First World War found it almost impossible to realize how short a period was required to do away with free values and attitudes. For those who thought historically it had become axiomatic that our modern age had established liberty as the indispensable basis of civilization. Experience in Germany since 1933 has shown that this basis can not merely be eradicated from the social and political structure but that it can be removed from the general frame of mind of the people. For many at this period freedom had lost its character of a value and was even regarded as contemptible bourgeois selfishness. It will be no simple task to redress the balance since twelve years of power and imposture have penetrated deeply, far more deeply than an optimist pedagogy would ever conceive. True moral attitudes cannot be taught by words; they have to be implanted alive in a favourable atmosphere and then encouraged to grow, and conditions since the war have provided little opportunity for that. To conclude, we should not forget that the ethos of freedom could be destroyed so easily only because there existed powerful tendencies in the whole of our modern situation, tendencies towards group existence, a planned and transformed social structure, which came to regard the free attitude of mind as disorder and opposition. For this there existed some justification. The kind of liberty which then existed and still exists was the individualism of the nineteenth century which had developed under very different conditions and found it extremely hard to fit into the new circumstances. There was, and is, a temptation to equate this earlier kind of liberty, characterized by individual inclination, with freedom generally and to repudiate it in the name of organized society. Here are some of the new problems for the educator.

They point in the following direction. The old free outlook was
14 based on the will to individual action. This also presupposed the modern sense of personality and its quality of initiative, the world as a field for free activity, and finally, the fact that only to a limited extent could life be rationalized and reduced to techniques. Under such conditions the attitude was the right one and it has produced most of what we recognize as modern culture. The best expression of its relation to society is still the formula of *contrat social.* People realize that liberty unchecked must lead to chaos. Consequently, each one contributes a portion of that liberty, sufficient to create an institution for the preservation of order, the State. Freedom belongs to the individual; the State establishes its limits. It follows that the devotee of liberty leads his real life in detachment from or even in opposition to the State.

Now the situation is somewhat altered. The earth has been fully occupied, there is no more empty space. The structure of social and economic life, comprised within the State, has grown steadily more massive and with its various instruments and techniques has embraced every department of life. To this there corresponds a change in man himself. What used to be termed "personality," the original element in a man's growth and development, is no longer universally accepted as the standard of a worthwhile existence, and besides, in comparison with the years before and immediately after the First World War there are far fewer original individuals or styles of life. Types and schemes have worked their way into the being of the individual, with the consequence that individual initiative loses its paramount importance. Collectivities have increased in significance and they are now the decisive factor.

That is the situation from which we have to start. The individual and in particular the man determined to exercise his freedom must not merely accept the modes of group life included in the State: he must give them interior assent, bear them in his mind, and make them his own.

He must look upon what is "public" as an object of private responsibility and decision. But this co-operation must proceed from a motive different from that which previously encouraged people to take an interest in the State; it has to come not from an individual zeal for work or thirst for power but from the objective and factual requirements of the whole situation.

It is important to realize that this primacy of the "whole" which has gained prominence in our historical development can be achieved in different ways. First of all, in what the experience of recent decades calls totalitarian. This primacy was never inwardly accepted by the still-considerable section of the body politic that was sensitive to individual values and therefore in opposition to it. Its main support is found in the masses whose significance this other section has not yet properly grasped and which must first establish its own position. In consequence, the attitude of the modern State today easily assumes the character of power. Yet this is not an essential feature and it should be merely a transition to a further state of mind that will develop in proportion as the whole populace gives its inner allegiance to the new State. Nor should we forget that to this power aspect of the State there corresponds an equivalent condition of mind in many individuals: a depersonalization as a revolt from oneself, the flight from responsibility, pleasure in subjection—itself, too, a defective outlook which needs to be overcome.

The true form of the future State will be one in which freedom will stand in living relationship to the groups that will come into ever more striking prominence. To bring this about, the individual must fit into their framework and functions, and abandon that reserved individual sphere and liberty of movement that were formerly possible. But at the same time he must play a personal part in them and not be caught up in them merely as an individual. There needs to be a blend of objective reality and individual collaboration—a blend which is already making itself felt at a number of points but does not yet dominate the whole picture. The growth of this new mental attitude will be assisted by another factor that provokes merely a negative reaction in a person who refuses this obligation, namely, the loss of originality, the readiness of present-day man to accept a scheme of things, which we have been discussing. This will allow him to adapt himself to the community without feeling, as the confirmed individualist must inevitably feel, that his freedom is being repressed.

It is not possible to work out a detailed programme. We are dealing with a living form which can arise only from living experience. In our case "life" does not begin with the fact that the individual demands guarantees for his personal liberty from the different groups but with the fact that he is genuinely determined to be free. Social groups, left to themselves, always follow the easiest path, which here means that of forcible administration. The individual has to create a field of freedom for himself, a task that calls for courage and a readiness to make sacrifices. But for a large number of persons the need to adjust themselves to the community coincides with an inner disinclination towards free habits. Dread of responsibility, an avoidance of understanding and decision, a lethargic refusal to stand on one's own feet, the whole flight from personal existence—these were all justified on the grounds that they were an adaptation to the community and they ended as a mere series of functions. All depends upon our realizing that this is not the true attitude of mind of the coming age but merely a distorted form.

More than ever must the individual will himself as a person, grow in power of judgment, act with a clear conscience, and accept responsibility for the consequences, not as an individualist or with wild enthusiasm but in an orderly and objective manner. He may, indeed he should, criticize, advocate sounder policies, and offer opposition, not directly to the groups themselves but making use of material from their substance, their interior reality. This is a more difficult task, demanding more understanding and effort and presupposing a rarer blend of qualities than in the battles for liberty in the nineteenth century. Yet it will succeed in the measure in which the will to freedom allies itself with the inner requirements of a genuine community life. It will gradually be made clear that the State, conceived as power, is in the long run an impossibility because, while the State is not a machine, it is also no heap of termites. It will be obvious that mechanical and biological functioning provides no suitable solution. Indeed, it would not function effectively. Friction would continually increase and its mistakes become more disastrous and more evident. By its very nature, the State has an orientation towards the human person whether its temporary rulers desire this or not. From this derive certain immanent and necessary principles to which the individual must conform.[7]

Up to the present we have been describing psychological and formal freedom, or, in other words, the nature of a definite form of act and attitude which experience discovers in our interior life. We have not yet touched on the contents of these acts and attitudes. Considered in its nature, free activity can be genuine or false, constructive or destructive, valuable or worthless.

What—it must now be asked—is the content of free activity? Does the whole process of freedom consist in the kind of operation described above? Is the operation indifferent to what is actually done in free initiative or does it also depend upon realizing acts of a definite kind?

---

7. Whether this proper form of the "total" State will ever be realized may depend on yet another factor that manifests itself in the modern outlook, to wit, a genuine anarchism: not the revolt of antisocial elements against the social order but the struggle of the person with his conscience and dignity against a State that fundamentally ignores them.

18 FREEDOM AND THE CONTENT OF ACTION

Freedom in Act and Freedom in Content

Freedom in act signifies the mysterious reality, contradicting all rationalist explanation and yet impossible to gainsay, that man, though he is part of the general pattern of Nature, represents in addition a genuine starting point, a beginning of movement, an origin of events, and a source of the process of becoming: not like a seed that introduces a series of forms of biological growth but is itself the product of a previous individual of the same species and is thus only a phase in the history of that species, but in a way that is unique and at once significant and hazardous. Consequently, being itself starts afresh with every man, and this new being is continually realized throughout his life in each truly free act. This tells us, however, nothing about the content of this beginning or of the act proceeding from it. Up to the present our arguments have only shown *that* freedom exists and *how* it is experienced. We have now to inquire into the *purpose* of its existence, *what* it achieves, and *what* is the contribution of the *free being* to this realization.

In general, the answer is that the free act derives its full validity from the fact that it is not just any kind of act but the right act. The phenomenon we know as freedom is realized only in right action in concrete circumstances. Of course, this experience of freedom includes another factor, a readiness to pursue mere inclination, a delight in what is purely arbitrary, which rejects this standard. But such an attitude of mind is at once seen to be in contradiction with and in revolt against what is properly valid. It may have a positive value in certain transitional or borderline cases with special psychological conditions as, for instance, at the close of a long period of entrenched tradition that has cramped every department of life or after an era of oppression by a government without any sense of moral responsibility. But normally, a man cannot adopt this arbitrary attitude except in bad faith, conscious that he is thereby destroying the true character of liberty.

The inquiries which follow are intended to show how the significance of the free act through right action is revealed in the different realms of existence.

Freedom in Immediate Sentiment, in Experience of Nature, in Relation to Things and to One's Own Body

The first stage of freedom in terms of its contents would appear to be that of immediate feeling. Whatever the affective response to his surroundings, as long as it is a genuine response, it means that the person concerned has broken loose from his self-awareness. He forgets himself; his attention is caught by the object which has stirred the feeling. At the same time, as if from a reverse direction, he reaches a more profound consciousness of himself. He achieves unity without introspection, simply by living experience. All true joy, every genuine happiness through things or happenings, and even every shock and pain that has been truly felt, brings a particular sort of liberation.

Conventional existence regulates feelings. A strong feeling is no advantage to the economy of individual or social life because it consumes too much energy and interferes with the "functioning" of the social machine. We therefore control and suppress, in the first place, its expression and then the sentiment itself. The result is a lowest common denominator of feeling to permit life to proceed with the least possible friction. Social culture to a large extent consists in this suppression and control of feeling. But in the process the original experience can easily be set aside, if not destroyed, and there emerges a state of repression and unreality. Quite apart from its content and by its sheer affective power every intense experience shatters this condition of things and releases what has been dammed up inside. It encourages individual life and assists its expression. It carries the individual feeling into the stream of common life and on to the wide ocean of the world. All this is freedom, accompanied at times by a sense of wonder at events, and our first impression may be one of pure destructiveness like some great suffering.

We must not forget, however, that this experience of liberation is ambiguous. It proceeds from feeling as such and gives no information about its ethical character. It can spring from unworthy and base feelings and provide a justification for them which they do not merit. The danger may be observed in the late nineteenth-century claim to "self-expression" against bourgeois views that has now become a commonplace; or again, at a higher level, in the ethics of good intention and sincerity that were in conflict with concepts of objective legality at the same period. This system rejected the objective truth and the regulative binding force of Right and placed the whole emphasis on the original quality of the act.

A similar liberating effect of feeling is found in a return to Nature. This has a particular element of genuineness and simplicity, in a word, of "naturalness." "Culture" signifies a transformation of immediate life and reality through spiritual claims and values, and this involves a degree, at times a very high degree, of the unnatural. The sense of immediate existence is disturbed, natural impulses become confused, beauty is damaged. But no sooner has a man turned to natural objects and processes than the natural element is released in him: he has a feeling of liberation from what is artificial, counterfeit, and debased that can soar aloft to a consciousness of rebirth. History bears witness to this urge towards a renewal through Nature, that tends to express itself at the close of a highly developed but gradually hardening civilization. We may call to mind Rousseau after the *ancien régime*, the Romantic movement after the *Aufklärung* and the age of court etiquette, and the Youth movement in reaction against the bourgeoisie at the turn of the twentieth century. Of course, as always occurs, this experience can equate the "natural" with what is merely part of Nature and play the traitor to the spirit. Further, man's nature is certainly not "natural" in the sense of something original and balanced. It contains many warped and destructive elements, not only at superficial levels that have been corrupted from without so that, as the Naturalists always suppose, man need only penetrate to his essential core to reach what is original; they are found at this core itself. Man's being is not, and never was, part of Nature; it is historical, that is, determined by spirit and personality. It did not commence as an unconscious and instinctive natural entity, from which a spiritual and personal existence has been gradually developed; it began with a decisive act which has influenced the whole of its subsequent history. Foreshadowed in many a myth and made clear in revelation, this decisive act was one of guilt. Its consequences have permeated to man's roots and corrupted them. Man does not have and has never had an innocent relation with Nature; it is profoundly ambivalent. In consequence, surrender to Nature instead of purification and balance may produce their opposite;

In this return to Nature is included also an element of infinity. What characterizes also distinguishes. Delineation is always a limitation; individuality, too, involves commitment. As soon as a man turns to Nature, goes down to the sea, climbs mountains, or is conscious of the spring, he senses the expanse of space, the immensity of natural forces, the boundlessness of life as a whole. This experience liberates him from the pettiness of his narrow individual existence and it can rise to that sense of the grand totality of things expressed in the poetry of the *Sturm und Drang* and in Beethoven's music. But it can lead as well to negation, and the man is overwhelmed, disintegrated, and intoxicated. In consequence, a man's sense of form and outline in spiritual personality, personal honour, and historical responsibility is loosened and eventually lost.

From these sensations of freedom we pass on to that of concrete things. I feel myself particularly free when I do correctly what I have to do, when I understand the thing in question, as it really is, and deal with it accordingly. The simplest instance is that of a tool. If I don't understand its purpose and apply it wrongly, it gets in my way. It interferes with my physical activity, disturbs its functioning, thwarts or confuses the working pattern which is composed of body, tool, the object that is being worked upon, the directing idea of the work, the relation of means and ends, the situation and atmosphere. This is summed up in the simple statement that I am not free in the employment of the tool. As soon as I do understand its purpose and handle it correctly, it fits into the complex of my plans and into the functional system of my limbs and organs. Spiritual purpose and organic activity pass through it unhindered and even develop in it. I become free in my contact with the thing and my use of it. When the tool has a functional structure with its own source of power, it becomes a machine. This does not automatically adapt itself to the working pattern of the individual, and the difficulty grows with the machine's size and complication. Yet a harmony can be achieved as is proved by the relation of the skilled technician to the highly intricate machinery for transport, scientific work, delicate specialization, armament production, and the rest. Other machines, on the other hand, themselves constitute the central point of the operation and the man has to insert himself into their functional structure. This gives a new character to the problem; the man "serves" the machine. The question arises whether under these conditions it is possible to have a really free pattern of work.[8]

---

8. We cannot enter further into this question. It introduces the most urgent problems of technical existence. It is evident that men become the slaves of machines at every level of mechanization and degradation. On the other hand, we cannot ignore the possibility of subordinating even very extensive mechanical patterns to man's conscious direction.

All objects, relations, and processes have their essential principles, structures, and modes of operation. No sooner is man's attitude to them falsified than he encounters resistance, clashes with these things, and is made prisoner by them. This indicates that there is something more in him than Nature. An animal does not run up against such obstacles, or it does so only in its brief period of early development; it adapts itself rapidly to its surroundings and the interplay of instinct, function, and object continues with full assurance. Man, on the contrary, has to learn how to deal with things, he must gain an insight into their nature and familiarize himself with their structure. And according to the measure of his success, objects and systems of objects become channels for his life, activity, and creativeness. He fashions his immediate world from his own claims and capacities but also from the structure and potentialities of the objects. In it his individual being is established, firmly rooted, and expanding continually, and it senses that it has been led into an open land. Man is made free for meaningful action with external things and through this for the expression of his own vitality.

The same holds good of the relation to one's own body, which can be an impediment when it is clumsy or untrained, feeble, sick, or damaged. It is the root of many an inhibition or misdirection in the life of the spirit. Indeed, if the essential relation between spirit and body becomes hardened or breaks down, the association of interior with exterior that runs through all living expression—on the one side, of content of experience, feeling, outlook, and character, and on the other, of structure, gesture, mode of expression—functions only with difficulty or not at all and the body is felt to be a fetter or a fraud; or when appetites are badly coordinated, when, for example, they cut across one another, with the result that man's nature is in contradiction with his deliberate will, as can happen on account of false education, social prejudices, and unassimilated experience. This points to an important task of formation and re-formation. If this is successfully realized, the spirit learns to develop in the body without hindrance and this can issue in happy experiences of freedom, as is well known from the psychology of games and gymnastics, of convalescence and health.

Stoppages and interruptions can also be discovered in the realm of soul and spirit. Talents, let us say, are not developed and placed at the disposition of the spiritual will; negative elements, present in every character, destroy or interfere with the positive elements; one inclination jostles another, as with versatile persons who have no obvious dominant characteristic and have never acquired one by self-discipline, and in many other instances. Notice has to be taken of those tensions and contradictions that arise between the unconscious life, with its instincts and trends, its patterns and regulations, its stores of memories and experiences, and the judgments, decisions, and projects of conscious life. They can impede or even cripple life as a whole. This brings us to the wide field of neuroses. If a violent experience is not absorbed but repressed, an appetite not fitted into the total scheme but suppressed, some moral responsibility avoided and dissembled, unconscious tensions originate which again threaten life as a whole. If, however, they are recognized and properly handled, they are resolved; the person's structure grows in width and forcefulness, the various component elements find their due place within it, and a sense of freedom breaks through that may soar aloft into the religious sphere.[9]

In all this we are dealing with freedom which arises when life runs true to reality. But this presupposes a definite outlook: the will to see this truth, obedience to it, and the courage to make the venture. A man may do it violence thinking it will bring him fuller freedom, that of an

9. Cf. Guardini in *Unterscheidung des Christlichen* (1935), the study, *Vom Sinn der Schwermut*, pp. 497ff.

overlord. It has been remarked that every action, over and above its particular purpose or significance, dictated by the objective, has the added attraction of an exercise of power. As long as this is under control, mainly through respect for objective reality, it is good and a continual spur to action. It can, however, grow too strong, assume an independent status, and thrust aside the claims of the objectively real. It can even take a special delight in revolting against these demands of reality, that of dominion in the extreme sense, of forcible action and cruelty. But this freedom is a specious freedom and its falsity provides a ground for the vanity of a bogus culture, the danger of false asceticism, and the sterility of rule by power alone.[10]

True dominion is rooted in obedience to the nature of things. The true master is the man who, guided by higher purposes, is able to fulfil this service in sovereign form. Reality acknowledges him and surrenders itself to him.[11]

This freedom is preserved in its integrity only if the relation to things and to one's own body is a balanced one. Things have a very insistent reality, with the consequence that a man sensitive to and caught up in their mode of being may regard it as the only real realm of existence and thus forget the spirit. In this case, he becomes their captive and their width contracts to a constricting narrowness as does that of the body as soon as a man, deceived by its physical vigour, looks upon it as what is

10. There remains of course the question to what extent this unnatural element derives from man's fallen condition, and this must accordingly affect all formation in ethics and religion. A false Idealism is optimistic and overlooks this. As a result, it does not bring reality into full focus and in the end it fails. In his *Pensées* Pascal has said cruel but true things about this element in existence. Cf. Guardini, *Christliches Bewusstsein, Versuche über Pascal* (1935), pp. 121ff. [English translation: *Pascal: A Study in Christian Consciousness* (Providence: Cluny, 2022).]

11. The classic example of a system of behaviour based upon the truth of being is found in the ethics of Thomas Aquinas, which in its turn adopted the ethics of Aristotle and has thus preserved an important heritage from antiquity.

exclusively real and living, as so frequently happens with the fresh discovery of the body in gymnastics, sport, and physical culture. We then find so cloddish an enslavement in spite of all health, physical beauty, and development that by contrast the awkwardness of an untrained body is insignificant.

Freedom in the Realization of Values

This experience of freedom has its counterpart on a higher plane in the realization of what are termed "spiritual" but are really specifically human values.

Knowledge, for example, means, to begin with, that I become aware how reality exists from a particular standpoint, how it acts and can help or harm me, and how I have to deal with it: an understanding which enables me to have that true correspondence with the things we have been studying. It further denotes that I understand the nature of this reality and grasp its significance. This is the object of knowledge, properly so called, and when it is rightly appreciated it should be desired not for any practical purposes, however insistent, or for an intensification of life, however lofty, but only on account of its high intrinsic worth. One very disastrous error of recent times, propagated by Nietzsche and Pragmatism, was the belief that truth consisted essentially in its effect upon life, in so far as it imparted to it assurance, energy, and intensity. According to this theory, thought which assisted life was accepted as true; what impeded life was rejected as untrue. And so truth was subordinated to life and its essential character was lost. But truth contains its significance within itself in its intrinsic validity and dignity. Truth is not utility; it is precisely truth. And it is here that we discover the genuine "utility" which truth does contribute to life. It is of decisive importance for life to attain to something, not subordinate to it but to which it must on the contrary adapt itself, and adapt itself not to its power or its convenience but to its excellence. If the man who seeks knowledge acts in this manner he attains to the realm of truth. So long as he does not have the knowledge, being remains nothing more than what is close at hand; its significance is a closed book.[12] Worse even, if he mistakes falsity for truth and is thus in error, reality is confused and its specious meaning deceives him and leads him astray. As soon as it is properly understood, reality is focused in the light of its true nature and the realm of truth opens. The man who understands enters into it, draws to his full height, breathes, and develops. It is this self-extension, expansion, and consolidation, this release of the spirit in truth, which fills so splendidly the writings of Plato, especially the *Apology*, in which Socrates, sustained by this knowledge, can declare that death is now no evil, and the *Phaedo*, where Socrates makes the striking statement that in contemplating truth the knower is "assimilated to truth" and given a capacity for eternity.[13]

A like phenomenon is observed in connection with a work of art. This can fulfil different functions: it can, for instance, when ornamental or pleasurable, directly enrich life; as ceremonial, building, or monument, it can fulfil social purposes; it may have a pedagogical effect in instruction and education or acquire an economic importance in art purchases. But its real significance consists in this: that it fashions a world, in which the essence of things and, closely interwoven with this, the essence of the creative artist manifest themselves more purely and completely than in the real world just as the small fragment of the real

12. Translator's Note: Once again, it is difficult to bring out the force of the German words in this passage, *das Seiende* and *Vorhandenheit*, which I have translated as "being" and "what is close at hand." *Das Seiende* is what really exists but is understood only in and through *Erkenntnis*, knowledge. Until it is understood, it is merely *there*, "close at hand" (literally, *vor-handen*). (Trans.)

13. Cf. Guardini, *The Death of Socrates* (1948). [New edition: *The Death of Socrates* (Providence: Cluny, 2019).]

world, which is portrayed there, achieves a wholeness which symbolizes
28 the whole of being. The beholder enters into this tiny crystal-clear world and feels the wholeness that can never be directly grasped. He becomes interiorly more aware of his own being and is conscious of an influence from an even more profound reality. Here too there is freedom, an expansion of vision and being in a form that touches our waxing, struggling, and fragmentary life with the promise of some possible perfection.

We may discover yet another parallel in law. To begin with, it establishes a system to regulate the course of social life. As State law, it directly fashions the community pattern; as penal law, it punishes transgression; as civil law, it administers personal and economic relationships; as procedure, it lays down rules for jurisprudence. But its specific meaning is the worth of Right as such. We have here, if not an identical case, at least a relation parallel with that of truth which we have been analysing. The proposition, "What benefits the people is right," is just as false as the proposition, "What advances life is true." To be sure, the rule of law ought to be decidedly "useful" but for the reason that it makes Right prevail. The proper "utility" of Right derives from the readiness of the community to accept it as superior to itself: firstly, in so far as law receives an inviolability that it can receive in no other way, and secondly, and in particular, because where "Right prevails" the community lives in the light of the Right. If men assert the supremacy of Right and carry it into effect, perhaps at cost to themselves, they experience a special release and expansion of spirit. They have a free open space in which they can exist with honour.

More could be said at this juncture about education and the healing art and kindred matters. But we must not ignore a possible danger. The importance of these things is so evident that a sensitive person might be tempted to look upon them as autonomous and to see in them—in "culture"—the ultimate meaning of existence. From this arises the cult of culture. This realm of values appears to men as the last and loftiest realm. Put more concretely, the realm of values, which ought essentially to be open before God, becomes enclosed and being is shackled by a new necessity.[14]

Freedom in Personal Relationship

A further form of freedom—personal freedom—is revealed in one's relation to other men as also to oneself, and it has a double aspect.[15]

Firstly, freedom of communion, experienced when I enter into a proper relation to another person, appropriate to him and to myself. An animal is congruous with its being developing only in so far as it grows to its full stature, afterwards to decline and die. Man, on the contrary, is made for *encounter* and he realizes himself in meeting his fellow men. This encounter is more than the contact of objects or animals with one another, which gives rise to a mutual interaction determined by existing circumstances. Man's life also is continually affected by this sort of contact, from clash and accident to the most complicated events in the social mechanism. Encounter means, however, that a man confronts a thing or a living being, especially another man, sees its or his structure, feels the force of its or his character, and is affected by its or his value. I can thus encounter the sea or a tree or a man, previously unknown to me, or one with whom I have long been familiar. I am then "touched by the light of its being" and affected by its influence. This relation becomes complete when the other man also has this experience of encounter and of encounter precisely with myself. You then have the mutual relation of the determinant and the determined. Accordingly, man is not merely linked in mutual contact with other beings; he has the capacity

---

14. Cf. below, pp. 70, 122ff.; also Guardini, *Welt und Person*, pp. 1ff.
15. Cf. Guardini, *Welt und Person*, pp. 104ff.

for encounter and realizes himself as this finds expression. His existence
30 is directed towards things and persons other than himself, and in the measure in which this outward orientation develops, so does he realize himself afresh and more intensely.

Viewed from this standpoint, self-concentration once again leads to self-imprisonment, which is broken down only through encounter. When men encounter one another, there arises a union which is more than the sum of the individuals who compose it, for instance, comradeship, association in work, friendship, love, various family relationships, the association between the teacher and the youth in process of formation, or between doctor and patient. Each of these unions has a value pattern of its own. The more this is brought out by the individual, the more can he break loose from self-enclosure and isolation. When, by creating this personal relation to the "other," a man enters into community and union, he awakens to his genuine "self." Love is the most intense form of this experience of freedom. It brings home to the lover the paradox that, while he was purely self-centred and belonged exclusively to himself, he was not properly "himself." But when he emerged from himself and the other assumed an importance greater than his own affairs, he then received his true being from that other.

To be sure, a danger lurks in wait for us here, that of succumbing to the direct influence of the other—not facing him in the living polarity of person to person but becoming a mere element in his entourage, in the system of his needs and ambitions; in such a case, both the genuine "Thou" and the genuine "I" are lost.

On the other hand, there is another kind of freedom to be found in solitude. This, too, is essential. Where the whole life is determined by the community, man is robbed of his responsibility and his humanity. Personal life is stifled when communities take control of power, and has been so frighteningly proved in recent years. The whole of existence is exposed to the public gaze, to be supervised and directed by public officials. Initiative is extinguished by the regulation of all forms of life, for a standard form is provided for everybody. Man loses the capacity to subsist in himself, he becomes just a cog in controlling mechanisms. Man needs the opposite polarity to community, namely, solitude, in which "he comes to himself." Man's ego is not ready-made like the concretion of an animal; he has continually to make sure of himself, to challenge himself, to form himself. This happens in solitude. This means not only that no one is there except myself; it indicates the possibility that I enjoy of turning and coming to myself, of standing up to myself, examining myself, accepting responsibility, and giving direction. It is in solitude that a living centre is established in a characteristic way. It cannot be localized in body, soul, or spirit, yet it is an object of experience since positive and organic radii converge upon it from all sides. You can never say it is here because it is immediately somewhere else, "between" the observer and what he is observing; for all that, it is there and it determines our mode of observation. It would seem to consist in different acts of relation, control, and command which are continually building the unity of the soul's life. But the unity they seek to construct they can also destroy, for example, through specious forms of force and regimentation, unless these are already controlled by the living centre, that is superior to them. Much might be said about this phenomenon of a centre, how to sustain and deepen it as well as its dangers and its possible destruction. Solitude in any case is a necessity essential to it. Where a man lives entirely with others, he loses this centre and becomes a mere element in other patterns.

Solitude, when properly experienced, may be seen as personal liberation. Its power and necessity increase with the stature of the individual, and he has all the greater need of it when his special talents are of an active sort. One condition of a healthy life is that this experience of solitude be constantly renewed, to some extent by every man and, in a representative sense, by certain individuals for all mankind.[16] Solitude stirs an awareness of his personality in a man caught up in a network of community relationships. It makes him conscious of his own centre, which at times is the centre of the world, that is the real world: not the mere complex of available objects but of the "reality" in which these objects are experienced, known, and accepted by the person in question. Then what has been said previously about the individual centre is carried over into the whole of existence. He experiences his uniqueness, which can be neither replaced nor displaced. And this has nothing to do with selfishness or self-aggrandizement. It is the foundation of man's being and worth—of the individual who, as a person, can never be a means to a further end and also of groups which, because they are human, can be formed only of persons. We have the obligation of penetrating into solitude, into the realm of "myself with myself alone," and it is often extremely difficult to do so, because it brings a man face to face with the forces and tensions of his interior life, with the exigent demands of conscience, and again with that particular void which renders association with the self so arduous and even unbearable and makes any exterior activity which distracts from it a welcome relief. I say nothing of the temptation of self to exaggeration, illusion, fixation, and obsession, about which pedagogy as well as psychology provides copious information.

Finally, genuine solitude can be achieved only "in the presence of God." If this is forgotten, the attitude changes to one of autonomy or exaltation and it heralds a further decline.

---

16. We may note here the preserving and healing functions of contemplative religious orders and also of those individuals whose life is inspired by the Augustinian theme: "God and my soul, nothing else is of significance."

Moral Freedom

We have already referred to another content of freedom which embraces all the rest and gives them their final determination, namely, moral freedom. It was always so, when there was question of what is right and of obligation. We must now examine it in detail.

Morality is the sum of what ought to be done, the good. This means in the first place, that it *should* be done, not *must* be done, and can therefore proceed only from freedom. Now all that is known as the "content of freedom" depends upon the freedom of action, even where what was originally done by instinct becomes gradually understood or what was imposed became accepted by one's will or where a habit was examined and approved. Here the decisive factor is objective truth, so that the freedom of act is required only in so far as it is needed to overcome interior oppositions, retain sensitiveness, and keep faculties in a condition to operate. Moral behaviour, in the proper sense, is realized only in the form of freedom though it must not be forgotten that a measure of freedom attaches to habitual action, so far as this is cultivated or at least not hindered, and even to a direct aptitude according as the will adopts a position towards it, forms or ignores it, develops it or neglects it.

This involves the further statement that good ought to be done, not because the alternative would be unpleasant or harmful but on account of its own worth. It is not subordinated to a biological or psychological instinct or to a cultural activity but to a particular responsibility of the person, his conscience. The matter in which good acts upon conscience cannot be summed up in the sentence, "If you wish to attain to this or that, you have to do this or the other thing"; it must be stated as follows: "This and that you ought to do, this and the other you ought not to do, absolutely and unconditionally." The summons of the good does not present alternatives and it offers no advice, it imposes a duty. But duty is the obligation that arises from the subsistent worth of the source of the obligation. Naturally, questions of purpose and convenience also enter, since the good is in consonance with reality and truth and, as such, capable of being understood by the mind and pleasurable to natural feeling. But, more fundamentally, moral obligation is related to the meaning of the good as such. In the last resort, a man ought to do good, not because it increases welfare, intensifies life, and develops personality but for the reason that it is good. The supremacy of good is what makes its claims and imposes its obligations.

What then is the good? The first and distinctive reply is that the good is something fundamental which can be determined by no other form of reality and no other value; it establishes itself on its own merits and is understood in terms of itself. It might be thought that the good is just truth as imperative, the essential truth of things and their relationships, requirements, and energies as a field for activity. This view would, however, ignore a central element in the problem, the unique character of the good. It would change it into a formal element, namely, the way in which the truth of the particular being makes its claim. But good is more than a form; it is, as will shortly be shown, something of rich and unlimited content and of absolute worth.[17] This special mark of the good cannot be derived from any other source; it is self-contained, rooted in its own high significance, and it imposes obligations through its own intrinsic worth.

Ultimately, the good is founded upon God. It is a Divine attribute; more accurately, an original aspect of His living Being, as also a direction of His living mind. God is the Good, in person, who declares and

17. Perhaps the finest achievement of the Socratic-Platonic philosophy was that it realized this with such directness and focused upon it so unerring an illumination. The same is true in the Christian tradition of Augustine. This experience is essential if we are to understand what Plato meant by Eros and Augustine by love.

loves Himself, the Good.[18] This Goodness contains a special note, that of the divine or, more precisely, that of His living Godhead which is not an aspect of a vague general numinosity but is His very self, of which we have knowledge only through His revelation. This note is holiness, once again understood in the genuine revealed sense. What confronts the individual conscience as ethically good is God's holiness in so far as it penetrates into conscience and makes itself an objective for man's action.

Man's character as man depends upon the fact that he is affected by the meaning of good and has obligations that derive from it. This fact is fundamental and neither can nor should be derived from anything else. To explain this obligation towards good by psychological or sociological conditions, to say nothing of biological suppositions, is to blind oneself to its significance. "Man" is the being who is obliged by good. No further "explanation" can be offered.[19] Consequently, the ability to correspond with the good does not in principle depend, as in the case of other values, on capacity and education; it is given with man's nature. It

---

18. This relation of moral goodness to God's essential goodness was suggested by Plato and fully recognized by Augustine. We should add that the widespread opinion that Augustine's *summum bonum* is a departure from Christian revelation distorts the whole notion. It is unfortunate when theologians without philosophical background pass verdicts on theological questions which presuppose a philosophical understanding.

19. It would be tempting to suggest that "the good" and "man" form a unity, in which the one is mutually determined by the other, and that this unity really constitutes a unique phenomenon. But we at once recall that "the good" is an absolute value whereas "man" is not; to include both in this relationship would be to introduce a relativity that would destroy essential differences. Nevertheless, there is a valid relation here, as will be seen, but only when the subject under obligation is proportionate to the obliging good, and this is in God. In His case the unity is actually realized. This may be expressed by saying that the sentence, "God is that being whose mind affirms the good unconditionally and creatively and whose being realizes it perfectly," is just as true as the other sentence, "The good is the value, which is affirmed unconditionally by the mind of God and realized perfectly by His Being." In other words, God's reality and will and the value of the good are identical. God is the living good.

establishes his meaning and worth and does this in an absolute manner.
36 Should he be indifferent to good or repudiate good as such, it does not signify that he is wanting in one disposition and has another in its place; it means that he has lost his fundamental character as man.[20]

On the other hand, it is evident that the Good is related to Being and its content. It needs it for its own development, in reality as in theory. Without the fulness of this content of Being the good would remain limited and inarticulate.[21] This becomes clear when we ask about its relation to creative activity. In itself, the good is unlimited in content and simple in form. As such, it has no immediate relation to concrete judgments and acts. I always know that I should do the good. The consciousness of being claimed and obliged by good is ever present. It may vary in kind and intensity, it may elevate or depress, encourage or discourage, it may be straightforward or complicated, stronger or more feeble, clear or obscure, but it is never entirely absent.[22] It is a fundamental element in man's consciousness and essential for both its soundness and its unity.[23] But as soon as I inquire in what good consists concretely here and now I receive no immediate answer. It is simple and must therefore unfold itself; it is comprehensive and has to be made more particular, in order to

---

20. We are not denying that there exists a special ethical disposition, a particular sensitiveness to ethical values, and a capacity for ethical formation.

21. This was also realized by Plato and described in a brilliant, if not entirely conclusive, way when he dealt with the relation of the good to the eternal Forms or Ideas which are the foundation of real existence. Cf. Guardini, *The Death of Socrates*.

22. That is, in no man, even the most criminal or degenerate, though it may assume very strange forms. We may perhaps be compelled to admit that the worst kinds of evil proceed from perverted impulses towards good.

23. There is an important subsidiary question: how the ethical factor in other value relations makes itself also felt, especially in knowledge. This is no mere question of characteristic phases such as zeal and love for truth; it is basic, so that we may ask whether, in the last resort, truth can be realized at all without the will to good. Plato and Augustine have formulated this question from certain points of view and denied its possibility.

provide the content of a practical judgment and act. This is determined by the actual situation. What obliges me is not good in general but the good incumbent upon me at the moment; more exactly, what is right here and now, and this "right" includes not merely immediate practical needs but the whole interior truth of things, man with his complete nature, and all of it envisaged against the supreme holiness of God. Consequently, the realm of values is realized in the claims of goodness.

Good action also signifies action that fructifies and enriches being. Good preserves life and completes it, but only when it is done for its own sake. Our previous remarks about the relation of truth to life are equally valid for the relation of the good. Pragmatism defined the ethical as that which increased life and therefore subordinated good to life. Quite apart from the problem of how the demands of life can be measured and in what a proper, worthy life consists, this interpretation would nullify the real service the ethical can give to life, namely, the erection of a superstructure of meaning, not subservient to life itself.

A moral attitude includes knowledge and recognition of this and a corresponding action. It is the source from which I experience my innermost freedom. When I realize that I ought to do something because it is intrinsically good,[24] when my chief motive, even though implicit, derives not from utility or pleasure but from the intrinsic goodness of the thing, then in that act I am free. It is characteristic of moral freedom that it expresses itself in detachment from the immediate self with its desires and in a movement towards pure obligation, frequently through conflict, self-conquest, and sacrifice.

This experience of freedom must be understood at different levels. There is, firstly, the fact that the burden of obligation disappears after

24. This insight can be communicated as, for instance, when I am not capable of assessing the matter in hand but accept the judgment of another man whom I know to be a good judge. This is one of the principles of ethical formation.

fulfilment. Then, obstacles and impediments, some of them deeply ingrained, are overcome and this is accompanied by a particular sentiment of victory and triumph. There is, too, an awareness of being in the right, in due order, in the realm of realities, and in truth. But, finally, there is another element belonging to the moral value. It is sheer breadth. To experience it is to enter into the liberty of the ultimate and decisive assent, the original freedom of the good, that can be defined only in terms of itself. Its measure will depend on the perfection with which the man acknowledges the demand of the good, the level of thought at which he assents to it, and the purity with which his action is transformed into effect, and this is "virtue." Its ideal limit, never reached on earth, is the man who not only acts with moral freedom from one occasion to another but who *is* morally free, has fought his way to a "moral nature," from whose purified being action readily springs forth as a happy matter of course, and then onwards to its fulfilment in the light of God, known in theology as *non posse peccare*, the impossibility of wrong action; and all this is based on the complete openness of the good, and with it man's nature finds itself in absolute harmony, and there is now no longer even an apparent inducement to do evil.

Direct feeling frequently suggests that freedom consists in the achievement of our own will. Pleasant and useful action appears as independence and so as liberty. But moral experience shows that this leads to a dependence on a self that has become a prisoner and on a determinist sequence of events; it may lead further to a warped condition and eventually to a typical and basic enslavement. What is misplaced, untrue, unjust, and evil belongs naturally to enslavement; it is the enslavement of the person who ultimately can breathe only amid the good and right. Effects of this kind follow more ruthlessly than those deriving purely from Nature.

The moral element can evidently be spoilt, for example, in the various forms of anxiety, one-sidedness, impatience, and pharisaism. Behind the acceptance of good are operative hidden motives, instinctive or spiritual in character—the desire for enjoyment, claims to importance and domination, obstinacy, often also inferiority complexes, uncertainty, fear—all of which make use of good as a means. Or it may be that one particular value exerts such a pressure on the will that a man loses his relation with moral values as a whole and fails to respond to other obligations equal in binding force. Moral energy can be switched to false tracks with a resulting distortion that can grow to be senseless and diseased. In that case freedom is lost and the width of ethical value is twisted into a servitude ever more oppressive and destructive.

These distortions, it is argued, justify the criticism of morality in itself, which occurs regularly in the history of moral doctrines and received its most radical form from Nietzsche. In contrast with a civilization which he regards as misdirected and corrupted by its ethical notions, Nietzsche paints a picture of man, rooted in Nature and sensitive experience, acting not from a conscience determined by good and evil but from the direct instincts of overbrimming life and natural creative energy. His ideas were put to the test in Germany during the twelve years of Nazi leadership and their influence cannot yet be fully assessed.

There is no such person as the man without conscience and morality, living in an "innocence of becoming and creativeness." Man's being and worth are established upon that attachment to good to which conscience bears witness. No one will dispute that difficult problems arise from this ethical obligation or that incorrect answers may affect the whole of a man's being. But it is equally certain that these problems can never be solved if man is regarded as a purely natural being; they have to be raised to the personal level as the foundation of morality. With all its refinement of psychological analysis and critical technique, Nietzsche's picture of man is, in the last resort, a purely primitive one and we can interpret it only as a sign of decadence if not of mental sickness.

Freedom in Religion

40 Religious experience and the act of religion provide us with one further type of liberation. Here the term "religious" is not employed in its Christian sense but denotes the experience and state of mind that becomes aware of and related to the divine, as generally understood, to the "numinous" as it has been called in the study of religions since Rudolf Otto.[25] The occasion and setting of this religious experience can vary greatly. It can occur in Nature, under the sky at nighttime or in the still mountains; it may be prompted by works of art, as when you walk through a cathedral or listen to music; it may be inspired by men of very impressive character; it can be caused by elevating or shattering historic events or amid day-to-day affairs; in fine, it can arise without any special environment, at any time, and from any direction; it can just happen. In such experience a profound level of man is affected. It is brought into contact with something other than the earthly and world-bound, an element at once strong and mysterious and yet profoundly familiar, which cannot be fitted into a known pattern, yet is actual and powerful and rich with meaning, essential for personal existence, and for which there is no substitute.

It took a long time to bring the religious phenomenon into focus or, perhaps more correctly, to refocus it, once it had been lost sight of in recent centuries. The eighteenth-century Enlightenment considered the essence of religion to lie in rational knowledge and ethical conduct. Nineteenth-century Positivism envisaged the problem historically and interpreted religion as the primitive form of understanding of being, which then progressed to a philosophical stage to conclude with the stage of the positive sciences. The Materialist view is that religion is superstition or, perhaps more deliberately, deceit, made to subserve social

25. Cf. Guardini, *Die Offenbarung, ihr Wesen und ihre Formen* (1939), pp. 7ff.

and economic purposes. In contradistinction to Rationalism, Schleiermacher tried to unveil the special character of the religious factor, and his opinions have been carried further in the philosophy and study of mythology of the Romantic movement. These opinions were repudiated by the Empiricism and Relativism of the late nineteenth century, and it required the discoveries of Rudolf Otto and the work of Phenomenology that followed them to bring out the original character of the religious factor. Since then there has been rapid development. Psychology now examines the structure of religious experience in both individual and community life, and this has been considerably assisted by the study of the unconscious and of myths. Philosophy tries to grasp the significant core of the phenomenon and inquires what is its importance for being generally and for personal life. Finally, theology is conscious that it must go beyond the oversimple formulations of metaphysics and fundamental theology, clarify the relation of this general religious phenomenon to revelation and faith, as understood in Christian teaching, and throw light upon the problems in that religion. The work that requires to be done is indeed overwhelming. Material from experience has to be more thoroughly studied, the meaning of the religious phenomenon more profoundly grasped, and false emphases and interpretations that have gradually accumulated from historical, psychological, and idealistic treatment have to be overcome.

Religious experience is no mere state of excitation; it is not a feeling without an object, nor is it a subjective function. It is a true state of apprehension, awareness, and certitude; in it something is "given" and the person who has the experience knows a definite object just as a man who sees, knows an object under the light. This object is real. It is related to the reality of this world, though it is not itself this-worldly. The relation can be felt in different ways: as creative, formative, permeating, and dominant; as filling, inspiring, fructifying, purifying, making blessed, as obligation, transformation, and promise; as anger, threat, judgment, punishment, absorption, annihilation—but always in such a manner that it reveals a significance of its own that lends a positive value to what might have appeared negative. Even numinous annihilation, properly understood, is but the expression of something unapproachable which exists in its own right.

The content of this experience is real, powerful, noble, great, triumphant, tender, interior, gentle, and individual to the point of exclusiveness, again all-comprehensive and yet able to reduce the diversities of existence to large unities. It may be associated with all values but it always remains distinct from them. Every true natural value can embrace it, introduce it into concrete existence, and make it part of life; yet it continues to be intangible and ineffable. It can make any existing being a centre of self-expression and operation but, in filling this being, it keeps itself apart from both its reality and its significance; it reveals itself as that which transcends every name. It hovers along the frontier within which an existent being defines and asserts itself as a self; it fashions the reality of this frontier, and therefore of this being, so evidently that we have the impression that it creates it. Yet at the same time it draws an absolute dividing line between itself and all existing beings, so that it might appear in itself to be absolute Non-Being.

From the experience and languages of mankind Rudolf Otto has described the special character and meaning of the numinous by the term "the Holy." He has in mind something original, impossible to derive from another source. It is significant in itself and it has significance for a man as soon as he wins a share in it. This share or association is "salvation."[26]

---

26. Translator's Note: The German text introduces a parallel between *das Heilige* (the Holy) and *das Heil* (salvation), which cannot be reproduced in English.

This element of "the Holy" is experienced inwardly by man—in his sentiments, heart, and conscience. But the mind immediately attempts to formulate it in queries and to express it by images.[27] There result the different religious teachings and systems: myths, cults, systems of education, religious philosophies, and the like.

If it be asked to what order of being the Holy belongs human experience and reflection answer that it is the Divine. But what is the Divine? What is its relation, in reality, to the world? We cannot pursue this question further except to underline the fundamental contradiction which presents itself at this point to the inquiring mind.

The first reply is that the Divine is the world itself or rather its mystery and secret, its "other side": what every element in the world is properly, if not immediately. It can be seen at the beginning of the world, as its source; at its end, as goal and fulfilment; interiorly, as its basis; it is always the ultimate essence of the world. This solution can be made more precise in various ways. Classical pantheism thought of the Divine as the original ground of Nature and the original force in history. Modern psychology regards it as the complex of interior images, proportions, and relations which control the personality and from the value of which its welfare depends. Nowadays we can discover a new interpretation influenced by ancient philosophy, Hölderlin, and certain trends in Existentialist and kindred thinking. According to this, the Divine is the way in which objects and events flash forth, revealing themselves for what they really are, coming into contact with the mind

27. Our analysis of the religious relation with the phenomena preceding it starts with immediate experience and then passes later to rational consideration. One could of course adopt the opposite approach and begin with the question of its origin and purpose, the significance and order of reality, etc. These problems would require to be discussed in themselves and would eventually find their real, living foundation in religious experience—a method neglected for so long by Rationalist metaphysics and philosophy of religion.

and assuring it of an ultimate meaning, at once clear and yet incapable of expression.

The second reply can be glimpsed and prepared by man but is seen in full clarity only through revelation. In this, the Divine is not a simple concept. We are certainly dealing with something original but it contains an ambiguity that cannot be resolved purely in terms of itself. To resolve it you have to start not with religious experience in general but with God, as He proclaims Himself in revelation and is grasped by faith. This God is not the world or man, not history nor existence. He is not the other aspect of the All or its mystery or its individuality radiating outwards. God is only and entirely Himself. He does not require the world for His existence; He would exist if there were no world and "nothing would be wanting to Him." But the world exists simply because of Him as preformed, created, sustained, and controlled. The "Divine" is that quality which belongs to it, now that God has established its nature and called it into existence, once God has brought it out of nothing and continually communicates to it. It is the quality it has now that God is within it, permeating it and drawing it to Himself, whether the world understand this or not; now that God directs history in it and pursues a purpose, whether the world co-operate or refuse to co-operate. The relation in which this sets the individual, the meaning deriving from it, the spirit breathing through it, the presence that can be sensed within it, the inner consciousness that draws everything from this, and what compels, obliges, and calls for decision, arising from this consciousness—all this is the "Divine."

Accordingly, it does not rest within itself but points beyond itself to God. It proclaims God and leads to Him. It puts the man touched by this experience into contact with the source from which he came and to which he is returning. This is where the ambiguity comes in. Man has revolted against God. He will not obey but wants to be his own master.

He wants to have the world, not on loan from God but as his sovereign estate. Yet the world is created and shows everywhere its mark of origin from God. And consequently, the man who refuses to acknowledge God has to deal with the Divine in another way: he attempts, as it were, to prize it loose from God and nail it to the world. He treats it as an aspect of the world so that it seems, in the twilight of time, to subsist on its own and to have its full significance from itself. For it is this numinous quality of the world which man, in the final instance, is seeking. This gives it its true value. Plato's notion that things have their real roots in the Ideas and that the Ideas receive their character as Ideas from the Good, the Platonic term for God, is one of the deepest insights of the human mind. Finally, only the Divine can "reward." The great temptation consists in laying hands on and wanting to seize what only God can bestow.

The true element in the Divine gives the man who senses it and lives by it all the values we have mentioned: in short, the experience of salvation. It involves a special kind of liberation, impossible to achieve in any other way. It may be felt in various forms: as a home-coming, a security, an inwardness; as a spreading of wings, a release into wide open spaces and a high ascent; as fulfilment in infinity and power; as an interior presence of goodness and grace; as purification, strengthening, and elevation. The experience may vary in intensity, in height, breadth, and depth, in richness and clarity. It may be original and yet be linked with and follow the experience of others. But it brings with it always the interior awareness of having entered into a realm on its own, which alone is real and alone enriches, into the realm of salvation.

Salvation denotes liberation from the cramped condition of individual existence, from its falsity and transience, its deceit and sorrows, its unworthiness and guilt. It is an entrance into the open land of freedom and fulfilment. The religious literature of very different peoples is full of this experience of freedom.

Yet this ambiguity in man's relation to God may bring with it a profound confusion. The most questionable and dangerous motives and impulses, and even the worst of them, may exercise an influence in religious life, as the term is here understood, and destroy freedom from within.

History and ordinary observation show us that the experience of religious freedom can be confused with feelings of liberation of quite another sort: with physiological stimulation, disguised psychical releases, or even in certain states of epilepsy and paranoia, with pathological phenomena. To these should be added those pseudo-religious experiences of exaltation, triumph, and transformation found in different varieties of Dionysus-worship and ecstasy.

At this stage a more fundamental query emerges, as to how far even genuine and direct religious experiences prepare a man for the freedom of the living God or can attach him to the world irrevocably because his interior motives are inextricably confused. The servitude indicated in the Scriptures by the "world," the finite enclosed within itself and resisting God (John 1:1–13), is ultimately religious in character. It can assume the shape of deities which link religious piety with Nature or with concepts of the All that bring God down into the world, or it may employ religious energy to deny and destroy the religious element. There is always in religious experience a latent possibility of imprisoning man within the world of creation and thus of converting freedom into its opposite.

Résumé

We have been analysing and tracing the phenomenon of freedom through the various regions of existence. Let us now take a glance in retrospect.

The same structure continually recurs. It has two centres of gravity. The first consists in what we have termed the freedom of the act: its manner, the way in which it is realized. Free activity does not appear in the free agent as events in the inanimate world do in objects. It does not arise from him as the movements of plants and animals arise from their organic and physical conditions. It has its origin proper in him, so that it belongs to him and he is himself in it. We do not at all ignore the part that may be played by interior disposition and exterior influences nor the fact that, as a rule, freedom can be only approximately achieved. We are examining the phenomenon itself. It consists in man's capacity to start an action on his own initiative and therefore to possess it and, through it, to possess himself. That the action is genuinely his is manifested in the way in which the agent relates himself to it, in responsibility. Freedom and responsibility are the bases of man's essential worth. To be sure, they present difficult problems to the mind and there is a great temptation to get rid of these by some short-term solution. Ultimately, the fact of freedom cannot be logically analysed; we can only show that it does not contradict a logic working on the right line and that such a logic can accept freedom into its system just as the real world is not only reconcilable with freedom but from its earliest elements onwards is orientated towards it.[28] Freedom is living, and therefore, like all living things, it must develop. But, in its quality of life, it is also free, that is, it must first be willed, it must build itself. A progress is accordingly possible—a realization through all we understand by exercise, self-conquest, and self-denial; there is the opposite possibility that it may remain undeveloped, deteriorate, and be smothered by instinct, automatism, and stupidity.

The second centre of gravity lies in the object of the free act. The first was expressed in the question how the act is realized, the second in the query what are the contents of such acts. These two aspects can to

28. Cf. Appendix at the end of chapter; also, Guardini, *Freiheit und Unabänderlichkeit*, in *Unterscheidung des Christlichen*, pp. 130ff.

some extent be dealt with separately. An action may be concerned with an object, even a bad one, and still be free so far as formal imputability goes. But in that case freedom is only half realized since it really implies both *freedom from something*, namely, from necessity, and also *freedom for something*, that, namely, which is right under the circumstances, considering the reality of being and the validity of values. Plato would say "what is right under the circumstances" and therefore with relation to the essence of the thing. Thomas Aquinas would understand "what is true under the circumstances," referring to the truth of Being, as expressed within the framework of the situation. This truth we have traced through its various phases and have shown how it is realized in feeling, in relation to things and to one's own body, to values, to other persons, to moral obligation, and finally in religion—in everything therefore that belongs to personal and objective culture. The act is supported always by psychological freedom, the initiative of responsible conduct, more or less clearly, with fuller or slighter awareness and decision, but always in some measure, be this only in the alternative possibility of not acting or of acting in some other way. When such an act proceeds as it should in accordance with truth, a field is immediately opened for free action. The agent has a sensation of release, of width, greatness, and value just as, on the other hand, that which runs counter to the truth, though for a moment it may be felt as force or intensification of life, is eventually cribbed, warped, and stifled and results in loss of freedom. This freedom is living, it should develop but it can decline. It too demands adhesion and a formation. It will be all the richer as truth is more clearly known, the right more genuinely willed, and its fulfilment springs from a fuller measure of decision and energy. Its dignity corresponds to the loftiness and worth of its object and the grasp it has of essential Being.

A man may do all he can to escape freedom. He may argue against it theoretically and in practice behave as though it did not exist and live merely by habit and instinct. None the less, it will continue to obtrude itself on him. The very escape and apostasy from freedom have the mark of freedom on them because freedom determines man once for all, and he remains free in spite of himself.

However, the possibility a man has of adopting this state of opposition to his own freedom presents us with a series of new problems. Where are the essential limits of this initiative known as freedom? What is their relation to man's finitude? How is human freedom related to that of God? There are other questions as well. Their importance is shown by the easy way in which philosophy yields to the temptation of equating human freedom with absolute freedom. For man may become intoxicated through his awareness of this initiative and feel he is master of it and, through it, of himself. Defective or diseased forms of living phenomena teach us a good deal about healthy forms. And so it is instructive to see how the significance of freedom is lost in the two false positions of Determinism and Absolutism. The former denies the existence of freedom; the latter identifies it with complete autonomy. The former reduces man to a purely natural status; the latter identifies man with God. Genuine freedom has therefore a complex character, not easy to determine, and one into which at the moment we can make no further inquiry.

The Subject of Freedom

We are now faced with the query: What is the subject of freedom? What makes it possible? What is the nature of that source from which it originally springs? What kind of being is it, that can be an individual, a person, and can develop this personality in a free act? The only answer is *the spirit*: not merely "the spiritual element" since that is omnipresent, and every being has its essential form and meaning, but rather a concrete-individual spirit as a subsistent reality. Why must I accept this reality and how should it be determined?

I discover in myself certain ways of acting, as when my body stumbles or my arm is busy working; these return to external Nature and their reality can be paralleled in the mechanism of external objects. Their subject is what we call matter or physical energy. I find other operations in myself—such as growth, material changes, the interplay of instincts—also belonging to external Nature, more exactly to the region of biopsychical life. Their subject is the reality known as life. Finally, I trace in myself other ways of behaving for which there is no parallel in the world of Nature by which I am surrounded: for example, knowledge by which I grasp the essence of an object; the creative act by which I transform an idea into concrete reality, and free activity by which I make a decision after due deliberation and am active in the world. In all these acts I step out of the immediate framework of my existence, detach myself from it, become conscious of the appropriate norm, and with it I make an inroad into reality; and this is true when I am dealing not with exterior objects but with myself. Such an attitude cannot be based upon a materialistic-mechanistic or a biological reality; it demands a being of an exceptional sort, which we term spirit.

What we have done was not to frame a concept of the spirit from some metaphysical preconceptions, in which case we should have to inquire whether it did really exist. We have stressed a fact of experience, namely, that what renders this attitude possible, is its subject and carries it through, is what we term the spirit: not merely "the spiritual element," what is logical and meaningful, for these are aspects of all being, but the individual spirit which as a person is in control of itself. It alone can detach itself from its own being and take up a position with reference to it. It can judge and take decisions. It can originate action, accept responsibility for that action and, in that action, for itself. To the challenge, "Who did that?" it can reply, "I did."

Without entering further into the phenomenology of spirit we may describe its characteristics as follows. It differs from the physical and the biopsychological and yet it is thoroughly real. In consequence, it has its relation to *Physis* (or Nature), builds up and controls the body, and reveals itself through it. Each part of the body expresses the spirit and in its turn affects the spirit. The spirit, however, transcends the body since it is always more than its bodily achievement and expression. The spirit depends upon the body in its functions though not in its essence and continuity; man's body, on the other hand, disintegrates without the spirit.

In itself, the spirit is non-spatial since it is wholly simple, but the body provides its position in space and time, its place of achievement and responsibility in history. It is situated in the world of things but it goes beyond it and at times may be in opposition to it. It thus stands at its margin and on its frontier, facing inwards or upwards.[29]

It is at this point that the spirit creates the "crisis" of the immediate world of Nature. It acknowledges and establishes it, serves it and uses it as material for its own activity and creation, and leads it into the historical process. Since its activity is based upon freedom and can make a false as well as a true choice, it brings it into a position of absolute danger. The spirit can succeed in passing from the first to the second, from the immediate world to its proper realm, but it can also fail to do so. The process can be properly fulfilled but it may also result in disaster.

When we assert that the spirit is the subject of freedom, we refer to the deciding factor in the subject of freedom, that which marks it off from subjects of other acts. More precisely, it is man. He is not spirit alone but spirit in matter or even matter in spirit.[30] In consequence,

---

29. Cf. Guardini, *Welt und Person*, pp. 28ff.
30. Guardini, *Das Auge und die religiöse Erkenntnis*, "Schildgenossen," *Jahrgang* 20 (1941), vol. 3, printed privately but with wide circulation (Berlin, 1941).

these two elements become somewhat altered: matter into body, spirit into soul. Both, however, are aspects of man. He is the being in which spirit is really incarnate, as had been explained; he belongs to the world and at the same time transcends it; he stands at the boundary of the world and is responsible for its "crisis."

Freedom is possible only where you have the individual spirit or, more exactly, the spiritual-corporeal man. He alone is capable of freedom and, it must be added, he is compelled to be free. Freedom is a dignity he has been granted; it is also an obligation laid upon him which he cannot escape. He is free and he remains free even though he does not wish it, even when he imagines he has convinced himself he is not free, and however strong be his sensation of being influenced and under compulsion, however advanced his tendency to drift and adapt himself to circumstances. The very denial of freedom presupposes freedom and bears its mark.

CHRISTIAN FREEDOM

St. Paul's Experience of Grace

Up to the present we have been speaking of freedom as manifested in direct human experience. We must now inquire what revelation has to say about it. Is there a freedom made possible only by God which must be called, more precisely, Christian?

The New Testament brings us into contact with a personality, Paul, who appears expressly as the prophet of the new freedom. The Acts of the Apostles and his own Epistles present him as a man of vivid personal experience and mighty will power, a man whose inner self was torn by contradictions and cramped by inhibitions. He had a passionate longing for justice; he desired earnestly and sincerely to be free and struggled for this freedom against very difficult obstacles. But his efforts must have prevented him from attaining clarity and liberty and he found himself more and more imprisoned in a way that had no outcome. Self-will was the probable dominant in these moral efforts and it brought about that constriction which we know as pharisaism. He failed to understand that evil must not only be combated but also overcome through wisdom and patience. Instead, he applied sheer violence to his instinctive life and it grew more and more infected. He gives us no direct testimony of this but, immediately he appears, he is confronted with an extreme crisis, and the way in which this developed and in which he subsequently spoke of it suggests that it did happen along these lines.

The Acts describes his contact with the earliest community of Christians. He is made aware of the life of these faithful, sustained by a mysterious spiritual power, their mutual love, the freedom and joy of the community (7:58ff.). He is present at the trial of the deacon Stephen and sees there the spiritual radiance mentioned in the text: "And all that sat in the council, looking on him, saw his face as if it had been the face of an angel" (6:15). From all this an existence is revealed to him, wholly directed towards God and containing nothing of that weariness of formal fulfilment of law, that tortuous struggle to achieve good by one's own strength, that futility and frustration he had been experiencing. In this desperate man it awakens a burning hatred. He assists at the stoning of Stephen and the destruction of the young community at Jerusalem. He accepts full authority to do the same elsewhere, and he journeys towards Damascus. On the way thither he has the momentous experience of his life. The Acts records it as follows:

> And Saul, as yet breathing out threatenings and slaughter against the disciples of the Lord, went to the high priest, and asked of him letters to Damascus, to the synagogues, that, if he

found any men and women of this way, he might bring them bound to Jerusalem. And, as he went on his journey, it came to pass that he drew nigh to Damascus. And suddenly a light from heaven shined round about him. And, falling on the ground, he heard a voice saying to him: Saul, Saul, why persecutest thou me? Who said: Who art Thou, Lord? And he: I am Jesus whom thou persecutes… Arise and go into the city, and there it shall be told thee what thou must do. Now the men who went in company with him stood amazed, hearing indeed a voice but seeing no man. And Saul arose from the ground; and when his eyes were opened, he saw nothing. But they, leading him by the hands, brought him to Damascus. And he was three days there without sight: and he did neither eat nor drink.

Now there was a certain disciple at Damascus named Ananias. And the Lord said to him in a vision: Ananias. And he said: Behold, I am here, Lord. And the Lord said to him: Arise and go into the street that is called Strait and seek in the house of Judas one named Saul of Tarsus, for behold, he prayeth. (And he saw a man called Ananias coming in and putting his hands upon him, that he might receive his sight.) … And Ananias went his way and entered into the house. And laying his hands upon him he said: Brother Saul, the Lord Jesus hath sent me, he that appeared to thee in the way as thou earnest; that thou mayest receive thy sight and be filled with the Holy Ghost. And immediately there fell from his eyes as it were scales, and he received his sight. And, rising up, he was baptized, and when he had taken meat he was strengthened. And he was with the disciples that were at Damascus for some days and immediately he preached Jesus in the synagogues, that He is the Son of God. (9:1–12, 17–20)

What has been happening? Paul is experiencing the reality of Christ, learning that the man whom the Jewish authorities imagine is dead and liquidated lives mysteriously on, is confirmed by God, and possesses dominion and glory. Paul opens his mind to this reality and believes. At once a shattering transformation takes place within him. He discovers the possibility of becoming good, just, and saintly, of a final fulfilment and liberty which cannot be achieved solely by a worldly approach and the application of human energies. He not only glimpses a new moral ideal; it is not merely that a new way of religious self-formation, hitherto unknown, becomes clear to him. The living God draws near to him in Christ and takes him in His own hands. Paul stands now in a totally new attitude of life which subsequently he will express in the often recurring words: "I in Christ and Christ in me." This does not imply that he ceased to make personal efforts. His Epistles prove the contrary. The whole force of his powerful will and vivid experience comes now to its full development in a manner different from before. This happens "from faith," in such a way that he trusts the God coming to him in Christ, leaves an open place for Him, and allows himself to be fashioned by God.

This signifies, to begin with, that God Himself is free. The words may seem absurd but they have their point. If we examine religious experience as a general phenomenon, God is not regarded as free. A little honest self-examination and reflection on one's fellow men and on history suggests that man's self-will, the inner forces that confuse and degrade him, his insincerity and violence nowhere operate so disastrously as in what is known in general as "religious experience" and "religious life." To be sure, the ultimate objective is God but God's image and God's claims are made subservient to man's own will. What appears a proclamation of the Divine will is often nothing more than man's way of establishing his own position. What claims to be the figure of the Divine is frequently an absolute hypostasis of one's own nature. This may seem

an impossibility for after all God is the Almighty but it is a consequence
56 of God's will that man should have his due initiative. But, if God is to be really revealed, He must emerge and remain there in objective form and speak with a lucidity which man's profound disloyalty cannot call in question. This is what happens in Christ. Within the framework of His personality and life God so manifests Himself that whoever sees Christ may be said to behold "the glory of the only begotten of the Father" and even "the Father" Himself (John 1:14; 14:9). Christ is the bodily epiphany of God; in Christ the hidden God emerges into the open light of history.[31] Paul's experience, which is repeated over and over again when a man believes, shows that the living God is not, in principle at least, held back by the selfishness and dishonesty of human nature and appears in the form of a human being.

Act and Content of Christian Freedom

This creates for the believer a freedom that is novel and irrevocable. As has been stated, the freedom that derives from the content of the act consists in a man's right relation to being; he senses the truth in its essential nature, notes the worth it incarnates, and makes a place for it in his life. Revelation now sets man before the richness of being and the supreme dignity of God, His truth and holiness. This can never be reached by man's natural forces; it is given him in revelation as the content of life. It is accepted in the basic Christian attitudes, enumerated by Paul in the thirteenth chapter of the First Epistle to the Corinthians, "faith, hope, and charity." They are spoken of in all the sentences about a share in the Divine life: the gospel of the kingdom of God, of the new man and new

31. How far the fact that God's revelation can be circumscribed or distorted by man's self-will means that God requires an organization which can present Him with proper clarity, namely, the Church, is a question that would take us too far from our present inquiry. Cf. Guardini, *Die Offenbarung* (1940), pp. 118ff.

world, eternal life, the heavenly banquet and the everlasting hymn of praise, of the love that never fades. It proclaims the conquest of all that is "old" in a never-ending "new," a decline and rebirth, a sensitiveness to and a capacity for the sacred fulness of God. Thus is liberation fully consummated—the entry into an open country that cannot be reached at the levels we have been discussing but must be opened by God Himself and that none the less can satisfy the sense of incompleteness which, Augustine tells us, God has placed in men: "Thou hast made us for Thyself, O God, our heart can find no rest till it rest in Thee."

In the Epistle to the Ephesians Paul speaks eloquently of this freedom when commenting upon the decree of salvation fulfilled in Christ and on the "boldness" and "access in confidence" that we have "by the faith of Him." He continues as follows:

> For this cause I bow my knee to the Father…
> That He would grant you, according to the riches of His glory,
> To be strengthened by His Spirit with might unto the
> inward man,
> That Christ may dwell in your hearts;
> That, being rooted and founded in charity,
> Ye may be able to comprehend, with all the saints,
> What is the breadth and length and height and depth,
> To know also the charity of Christ which surpasseth all knowledge,
> That you may be filled unto all the fulness of God.
> (Eph. 3:14, 16–19)

The thoughts expressed in the text and the massive structure of the single sentence, with the "breath of the spirit" blowing through it, reflect the grand spaciousness and the rich values, surpassing all finite measures, of this holy freedom.

The revelation of this special and ultimate factor shows the condition in which man and the world exist—that of sin. This denotes an opposition to God's holiness and therefore imprisonment in a final falsity and injustice. Even if all this-worldly truth and all earthly and human values subsisted, sin would drag them into the eventual disorder that encloses a man within himself and, despite all these possibilities of liberation, sets upon him a seal of final servitude. From this he can be liberated only through the revealed truth and love of God in Christ, and it is in the light of this full release that all previous liberations find their proper place. Augustine in the passage quoted understands by "rest" the significance, finality, and peace of freedom in God. It may be experienced also in the form of overbrimming and bursting forth and joy without limits, as we see from the passage of Ephesians, a veritable paean of the spirit.

So far as the second aspect of Christian freedom is concerned, that which is determined by the content of life—what is its relation to the self-dependent act? One reply is clear from revelation and faith. Gone is the illusion that man is capable of operating at this level, or that unaided he could embrace, attain, and grasp this. As soon as the believer knows Christ he recognizes his own powerlessness. Gone again is the false pretension that a man can fulfil God's demands with his own strength and the will's spasmodic and strained efforts to fulfil them. But this is already liberation. Paul no sooner recognized and accepted this than he must have felt an immense relief.

But—it might be urged—does not this involve a sheer hopelessness? That might be the case if God's revelation were only a manifestation and a claim. Actually, as soon as it does manifest itself, it gives a capacity to appropriate it; when it makes its demands, it provides the power to fulfil them. In revealing Himself, God gives the eye that beholds the truth, the courage to make the venture, the love that returns to Him. Paul's experience of this was so striking that it made him the particular prophet of this mystery. It showed him a power which made Christ knowable, brought Him within the soul, and associated man's innermost will with Him. The power that achieves this is the Holy Spirit; its force is grace. The spirit causes Christ to dwell within the believer, and the believer to dwell in the Lord; and this indwelling is not merely in the sense of knowledge and love but in that of life and being. This Christian doctrine of "indwelling" recurs continually with Paul. It is his final formula for redeemed existence. Possibly its most perfect expression is found in the Epistle to the Galatians, where he writes: "I live, now not I, but Christ liveth in me" (2:20).

This does not denote that in Christian existence the human "I" is blotted out, and that Christ enters in its place. It means that precisely because Christ lives in me, I am finally able to be *myself*—that *self* which God had in mind when He created me and there awoke in me my power of initiative, decision, and self-development. The mystery of this association becomes more evident in John's Gospel, where Christ says: "The water that I will give him [the believer] shall become in him a fountain of water, springing up to life everlasting" (4:14). The spirit does not so operate that it pours the Divine flood over a man, drowning his human ego, but under this sanctifying shower a source is opened in the man himself, that is wholly a gift, wholly a source of God's life, but it springs up in the man himself and thus belongs to him. It is the mystery of a sacred initiative that is God's gift and, for that very reason, creates what is most intimate in man. With this, the phenomenon of freedom passes over to that of grace, for grace is what God gives, but it becomes a more intimate possession of the man to whom it is given than the properties of his own nature.[32]

32. Cf. also later paragraphs, pp. 61ff.

What then in this Christian existence is the relation of human initiative to the Divine initiative? The question often recurs in Christian thought and the answers have been hotly debated: that of the Pelagians, for example, which places the principal emphasis on human initiative and leaves to grace the function of liberating, clarifying, and strengthening it. This solution is in radical contrast with that of the sixteenth-century Reformers, which looks on all human initiative as totally vitiated by sin and as having no longer any relation to God's holiness so that everything rests with the Divine initiative; all man can do is surrender himself in complete faith to God. This opposition has developed in a milder and more realistic form in the centuries-long debate between Molinism and Thomism. Both schools of thought firmly maintain that in the origin as in the continuance and development of faith God's initiative is paramount but nevertheless man, as man, is also active in making an approach to faith, taking a decision in the light of faith and living, persevering, and acting in faith. Within the one unity, however, the two systems define the character and degree of co-operation in a different manner; the former is more concerned about man's particular activity, the latter about the universal efficacy of grace. These discussions have brought to light important points, but in their attempt to settle the question of what scope and effect is to be attributed to the one or the other, they treat the Divine and the human initiative as entirely separated factors.

If we reflect upon the teaching of Jesus and the way in which He appeals to men and gives them responsibility, warning them to be humble and yet encouraging them, there is no doubt that everything of the order of salvation is grace, gift, and effect of the redeeming God; but there is just as little doubt that men have this relation to the omnipotent God with the full capacity and freedom of their being. It is impossible here to divide and measure; what is peculiar to this relation is the fact, which we shall examine subsequently, that man fully realizes himself and becomes free through this influence from God and that, on the other hand, God's activity presupposes man's readiness and develops to the extent to which man responds and collaborates. Jesus informs His hearers that God calls whomsoever He wills and gives as He chooses (Matt. 20:1, 16) ; but He makes it just as evident that salvation depends upon their decision (Mark 16:16); He puts before them the extraordinary challenge of the Sermon on the Mount, and the account of the judgment makes the judge's verdict on the significance of a man's life for eternity turn upon his practice of mercy (Matt. 25:31–46); it is quite in harmony with this spirit that we learn that He *could* work no miracles "because of their unbelief" (Matt. 13:58; Mark 6:5). Each of these aspects is true and they unite indissolubly in the one relationship in which God's initiative is everything and yet because of it man becomes free and endowed with vigour. Man is challenged to make his decision when confronted with the tidings of salvation. That the tidings exist, that he has heard them, that they have made their appeal to him—that is grace, and again it is grace if he responds and believes, but this decision is also his special act and responsibility. Jesus can therefore say: "Jerusalem, Jerusalem…how often would I have gathered together thy children, as the hen doth gather her chickens under her wings, and thou wouldest not" (Matt. 23:37). These two aspects do not exist side by side as in some external co-operation but they mutually penetrate, in the unbroken unity of one existential process. Similarly, the man is challenged to a life of faith and to realize after the pattern of Jesus a conversion of mind and thought and the transformation of his whole design of life and being. This can be achieved only through the power of redemption, as Jesus expressly declares: "Without me you can do nothing" (John 15:3); at the same time, these demands are made on a man's full power and it is his task through effort, self-conquest, and detachment to ascend to an ever-higher and more genuine realization of the Christian counsels.

Such a realization includes a growth in freedom of spirit and heart. This is what Paul has in mind, from one special angle, when he utters this warning: "The time is short. It remaineth that they also who have wives be as if they had none; and they that weep, as though they wept not; and they that rejoice, as though they rejoiced not; and they that buy, as though they possessed not" (1 Cor. 7:29–30). Here the believer becomes independent of all created things through the grace of God but also on account of his own courage, discipline, and sacrifice, in which he is wholly open to the truth and richness of God and is master of his own power of action.[33]

---

33. Spiritual writers speak eloquently of this freedom. Leaving aside better-known authors, I should like here to give an extract from a little-read writer. I am referring to the eighth chapter of the *Meditations* of Gerlach Petri (1378–1411), here translated from the German text of N. Casseder (Frankfort, Main, 1824), pp. 22–24.

"(1) Do you not know, says the godlike bride in the spirit of truth, that I have received the grace, after detaching myself from all images and representations, to stand, wholly pure and detached in spirit, in the presence of the eternal and immutable truth, of the Being that is always like to itself, that always is what it is, that alone in reality goeth out to all things and yet eternally and always abideth wholly in itself?

"(2) Nor is this all the godlike soul can achieve. She raises herself above all the forms of things and penetrates them, for she beholds in every created object what is divine and supernatural in it; she is not impeded by the temporal form of created objects, she remains pure and free; in perishable things it is not the perishable to which she looks nor their nothingness; rather does she discover God in all and every one of them, in the least as in the greatest; nothing therefore can easily harm her inner life or fashion itself to her disadvantage…

"(3) And this is holy and genuine freedom of spirit, in the first place, because she loves nothing in this world and seeks nothing—neither honour nor repute, neither her own advantage nor gain, whether temporal or eternal, because what she does out of duty and necessity is not her proper life, because she is not unduly attached to any object, nor does she long for and desire it, for she would experience no pain in doing without everything and each single thing that she at present seems to possess; truth needs nothing, and nothing decreases or darkens her light. And, in the second place, because nothing is difficult for her, she knows nothing of and fears no hardship, effort and pain do not frighten her.

The Eschatological Mark of Christian Freedom

Christian freedom signifies therefore that man comes face to face with Christ and recognizes in Him the living God who till then was hidden; he recognizes and accepts the call, passes across in faith into Christ's world, and shares in God's truth and life; all this he achieves through the grace of the Holy Spirit with no pretensions of his own, and at the same time he realizes his full self. For the rest, life on earth continues on its appropriate plane. Christian freedom introduces no element of magic or exaggeration; it is thoroughly realistic. All the facts of natural reality are still present but a new reality is operating in them, a new possibility has been and continues to be open. Everything earthly can be made a channel of transition so that "to them that love God all things work together unto good" (Rom. 8:28). The outlook remains a sober one, and it ignores nothing of the incompleteness, the confusion, and the narrowness of existence; but it hopes for fulfilment and has the courage to persevere.

It is thus directed towards the future, a future that does not simply emerge from history but proceeds from the same Christ who brought revelation. In the last resort, freedom like the whole of existence reaches outwards to eschatology. Christian freedom is no ready-made thing, it is in continual process. Even natural freedom, it should be emphasized, is not a fully fashioned apparatus but something living which has to be realized in continuous activity, formation, and self-conquest. The same is true, in its own novel way, of Christian freedom. We may apply to it all that Paul says about the new man who develops through the incessant

---

"And when these are not really present or have already passed, she thinks nothing more about them, has just as little fear of those that may come, and even less pictures them in imagination; if anyone blames or abuses or depreciates her, she is not distressed, she knows nothing of an empty and unnecessary shame; of all such happenings she takes for herself only so much as Truth commands or Himself shows her, and nothing further."

conquest of the old man and in a perpetual realization of rebirth, based upon faith and baptism. The new freedom continues to be concealed, denied, limited, and destroyed by the old existence, through sin, deceit, and confusion. Yet this does not necessarily mean, as extreme eschatologists imagine, that everything remains unchanged on earth and in time and that the new element can be hoped for only in a paradoxical faith in a very different consummation. This new freedom is already there, wakened into life at baptism and growing in everyday Christian life. But it remains imperfect and weak. It is shrouded in a veil of contradiction and it requires the final revelation and completion. This happens through Christ. The liberation will be fully achieved when Christ returns to put an end to history and to pass judgment on it—the liberation of man and, through man, of all other things.

Then the freedom now hidden and repudiated will be made manifest and the whole world will be drawn into it. Much might be added on this subject, particularly through an interpretation of the Apocalypse. Our inquiry must confine itself to Paul and conclude with a passage from the Epistle to the Romans which, like many another Pauline passage, contains in embryo what later is more fully developed in John:

> For I reckon that the sufferings of this time are not worthy to be compared with the glory to come that shall be revealed to us. For the expectation of the creature waiteth for the revelation of the sons of God. For the creature was made subject to vanity; not willingly, but by reason of him that made it subject, in hope. [That was the curse which followed sin; yet this curse was associated with a hope; so that the creature lived] in the hope that it also should be delivered from the servitude of corruption, into the [future] liberty of the glory of the children of God. For we know that every creature groaneth [with us] and

> travaileth in pain [with us], even till now. And not only it but ourselves also who have the first fruits of the Spirit [are not complete but] groan within ourselves, waiting for [the entry into] the adoption of the sons of God, the redemption of our body. For we are saved by hope. But hope that is seen [in its fulfilment] is not hope. For what a man [already] seeth, why doth he [still] hope for it? But if we hope for that which we see not, we wait for it with patience. (Rom. 8:18–25)[34]

The Relation of Christian to Natural Freedom

It would be logical to conclude these reflections with the question what influence the Christian attitude to freedom has upon the natural attitude and what its significance is for the development of personality and the furtherance of human activity. It lies, however, beyond the limits of this inquiry and cannot be treated in any detail. We must in consequence confine ourselves to a few thoughts and suggestions.[35]

There is no doubt that a serious, convinced Christian life develops a freedom of will and initiative. Relation to the living God gives to existence a permanent and effective support from which it can transcend itself. It breaks the spell of immediate existence: Nature with its forces, human society with its power factor, cultural life with the tyranny of its conventional standards. Interior obstacles are loosened, things appear in their true nature and significance, the strength of self-conquest increases.

---

34. The words in brackets are added by the author to facilitate the interpretation of the passage.

35. Were it to be treated systematically it would introduce the second part of the questions, whose first part is dealt with in "Natural Theology." This examines the factors in the nature of the world and man which point to what transcends the world and man, namely, God and the possibility of His activity. The second part, to which we have referred, would proceed from revelation, apprehended by faith, and consider its significance for the immediate existence of the world and man, and for man's understanding and explanation.

The real meaning of freedom, namely, to take possession of oneself through mastery over one's actions, cannot in fact be achieved except in dependence upon God. Man is finite and finite being denotes a being dependent on God. If man is not prepared to exist before God, then he either falls victim to the temptation of Nature and abandons his personal existence—to be ranked among genera and species or in the total pattern of the universe, where every form of Naturalism places him—or he emphasizes but exaggerates his freedom, giving it an absolute value and putting himself on a level with God, as happened in medieval Pantheism and continues to occur in modern philosophy, especially in Idealism.

This destroys the genuine bearing of freedom, which includes, on the one side, the courage to embrace real freedom with the obligations and risks that it involves and, on the other, a humility in finitude, possible only under and before God.

Modern ethics argues that when man obeys God's commandments he becomes heteronomous, belonging to someone outside himself, whereas freedom fundamentally consists in autonomy, in perfect self-dependence. But this argument understands freedom as absolute freedom and thus equates human freedom with Divine freedom. Were that the case, obedience to God would certainly take away human liberty. But in fact, God alone is God; man, conversely, is His creature. Man's freedom is a created freedom and it therefore develops essentially before God and in subordination to Him—all the more so since God is not only creator of being but also ground of truth and source of good. In consequence, obedience to God does not signify subjection to superior power but the fulfilment of what is right and good.

A closer examination of this supposed heteronomy shows that the argument is based on a serious misconception concerning God, possible only when a man has lost all practical contact with Him. The misconception consists in imagining that God is a ἕτερος, "an other." Normally, it is true that a being not myself must be an other so that if I obey him, I am obeying someone else. But this is not true in God's case and only in His case, and this fact determines His reality. God is not of course myself—such an assertion is the false supposition of Monism. This error is based on a misunderstanding of a truth, namely, that God is not "an other" but is that Being in whom my existence is established, my truth preformulated, and the significance of my existence contained. If I come to God in knowledge, love, and activity, I discover myself in Him. Obedience to God means first of all my acknowledgement that I am not in an absolute sense lord of myself and that the ultimate ground of my activity lies in Him, but it also denotes the overcoming of the foreign or improper element in myself. When I obey, I am acting in conformity with my true nature and so, rightly understood, I stand in my proper position within myself.[36]

It was previously asserted that freedom develops in a right relation to reality, in the realization of the true and the good. How is this affected by revelation and faith? Do these help man to attain to the essence of things? Do they provide him with power and assurance in that dominion over Nature which is his province and privilege? We here call to mind an historical fact often overlooked in discussions of the cultural value of Christianity, namely, that it was Christianity which first made possible the massive advance of Western man to that dominion. This claim may seem slightly strange since it has become practically axiomatic that man achieved freedom of knowledge and action only in so far as he emancipated himself from the shackles of Christianity. At certain historical moments this may have been true, for this advance was for the most part made in opposition to, or at least outside of, the clerical Christian tradition. None the less, it presupposed that tradition.

36. Cf. Guardini, *Welt und Person*, pp. 20ff.

The teaching and work of Christ first provided the believer with a status that was not one of imprisonment in the world and yet was operative within it, and in consequence with a liberty that otherwise would not have evolved. This was, in the first place, religious, but it penetrated into the whole mental and spiritual life. It gave man his inner independence of Nature, his capacity for adventure and enterprise which has been the source of the scientific, artistic, and technical civilization of modern times.

Man, who had lost faith, was still protected by the power and status that had been won in Christian existence. But it is highly problematic what will result from the efforts of this and the succeeding age, if the force of the Christian position and the protection afforded by the Christian system of life continue to decline. Modern man is often horribly primitive in his ideas about life. True freedom is highly complex, the result of initiative and obligation, a blend of the immediate moment and of tradition, of self-assertion and at the same time restraint. It presupposes order, external and particularly inner existential order. But does modern man exist within such an order? Till now he has always lived under the influence of the older patterns of life. In the measure in which these disappear he will drift into a chaos that is no mere lack of organization but a confusion of the fundamental elements of existence.

In earlier periods, in antiquity or the Middle Ages, man had his place in the immediate scheme of things. His control of Nature did not go essentially further than the potentialities of his physical and spiritual organs. The structure of Nature was not basically altered by him, and this gives the old culture its characteristically "natural" and "humane" spirit. This harmony with Nature and humanity vanished as soon as man learnt, through more exact insights and methods, to break up natural structures and to use their material and energies for purposes of his own. Another aspect of man now came into prominence, the "inhuman" man whose attitude to Nature is not one of reverence and obedience but of ruthless mastery; the older world disintegrated.[37]

Man has therefore abandoned what till now had been recognized as the foundation of existence and ventured into a land of wilfulness and insecurity. He dissolves and reassembles, adapts and constructs, meaning to be master of himself and of the world and to fashion a work that will not, as in earlier times, continue or adapt Nature's original patterns but will form an autonomous pattern from his own mind. He has cut himself adrift also from revelation. Its truth is no longer a standard for his life. And if, more recently, with reference to pre-Christian and non-Christian cultures and their religious expressions, he has begun to talk of "deities" and to look for a this-worldly religion, he forgets that all the deities we know presuppose the old Nature, not yet broken down through science or techniques, and man's corresponding relation to it. But are there other deities? In my opinion, once man, empowered by the freedom that redemption brought, has reached a full control of Nature, no more deities are possible.[38] All that is left is the choice between the

37. This makes the destruction of an ancient work of culture such a serious loss. It is at once the expression and the atmosphere of the "human" man and can never be produced by his successor. But this "human" man is part of the human totality and needs encouragement if he is not to collapse altogether. He contains the forces that preserve and heal man's nature; in him is centred the yearning for what is lost and the hope that it may be refound. He needs the older works and forms; they remind him of himself; they help him to come to himself. Their ultimate loss would not be merely aesthetic or antiquarian; it would be an existential loss.

38. It would appear that only original phenomena can assume some quality of the numinous. There is a divinity of the sun but not of an electric bulb; a fruit but not provisions; a river but not the chemical formula for water. "Deities" do not survive rationalization and technology; only the living God (be it said in due reverence) can do that, for He is Lord and Judge of both knowledge and technology. Or is one to suggest that a certain numinous element might show itself in a world of technocracy, in an autonomous realm of science, machines, and planning? If so, it would be absolute devilry. The numina of the ancient world existed in the Advent period; they could be employed in the revelation of the living God. Such a numen today would signify a revolt against the Lord of the world, a revolt impervious to all conversion.

living God of revelation and the self-divinization of man, standing there
70 in juxtaposition with Nature, unless even this attitude is to be regarded as a mere transition and everything would end in an unrelieved Empiricism.[39] But what if the creator and Lord of the world really exists and His creatures obey the dominion of man only as long as man acknowledges his own master? What if all this apparent mastery is purely arbitrary? Would not the nature of things and man's own nature take a frightful revenge upon him and, while he deems himself to be their master, reduce him to the status of a servant, perhaps even a plaything of their scorn?

These are questions ruled out by the dogma that man's glory is centred in himself. But man remains conscious of them interiorly, and specialists like teachers and doctors are beginning to warn men that they cannot act as though their existence were in good order when actually it is not. Man could aim at mastery of the world only because Christian freedom made him capable of doing so. It was right that he should do this; it was the task and mission of the new age. But he cannot carry this task through successfully unless he retains that freedom which guarantees his position and his true relationship to Being.

The realization of values, the conquest of reality, and the creation of some masterpiece are not simply to be explained as though a man were applied to the object like some readymade, effective instrument and he thereupon functioned. Man lives in this thought and conquest and creation; with impulse and desire, spirit and conscience, he passes from one decision with its consequences to another; he "exists." This means that this thought, conquest, and creation are directed by hidden forces within

39. This danger might arise not merely from a lack of religious insight and system of life but also because the religious forces that belong essentially to man and the religious interpretation of the world no longer found any place in which they might lodge. Man's mastery of the world would then mean that, in addition to a comprehensive rationalization and technique, there would be an unanchored numinosity active on its own and it would be impossible to foretell the consequences.

his existence, undreamt of in the naïve theory of progress. But what are these forces? How is the inner citadel of man built up?

All life that is determined by spiritual factors has one essential postulate, namely, a submission to truth, the will to do justice to the nature of things. Only on this basis does the eye see correctly, the action retain its proper order, and the work get done as it ought to be. Should this condition be absent, everything in the end goes wrong. But there is in man a factor that wants dominion, not obedience, not merely that dominion which is compatible with obedience to the Lord of creation but absolute power over the world, a dictatorship. This desire penetrates everywhere and it may therefore happen that an immense amount of knowledge, power, and achievement, a creation of fantastic dimensions, is accumulated and yet the whole of it is wrong at its inner centre. Indeed, this does actually happen. Modern man feels—consciously, if he is alive to it, or in the shape of a profound malaise, if he is not—that he is being damaged in every respect, in body and soul, in heart and spirit. He feels that the principles which explain life are not there, that relations between individual men are untrustworthy, that words are empty and his work is out of tune. He has a growing sense of being lost.

This is no cultural pessimism and no romanticism but straightforward truth and it would be very foolish to accept it as inevitable. Man cannot make further "progress" without asking what are the preconditions of the right kind of life. Since the First World War there has been a marked shrinkage in the field of man's existence; it has become capable of supervision and everywhere it calls for planning. But this "planning" signifies not merely that political, economic, and sociological resources shall be established and used in the right manner but also that men shall inquire what are the essential conditions of this proper life. The first of these is found in the primary truth that man is indeed capable, as the image of God, of ruling the world but in submission to the Lord of all created being (Gen. 1:26). Modern autonomy theories argue that notions like sovereignty over the world, providence, the judgment of good and evil, the establishment of moral values were formerly accepted as prerogatives of the Supreme Being but pass now to man, this world, and this earth. "God" was once necessary because man was not yet mature. He was the form in which man, still in his infancy, beheld his own power; that was the only way in which he could then shoulder it. Man has now grown up and become adult and "God" is simply the obstacle on the path to complete self-realization.[40] But what again if this be mere illusion and presumption? What if God really remains God and man continues to be man?

Further, it is not a question of a metaphysical theory out of all contact with real being but of the basic conditions for our actual human existence, conditions which permeate it even to the simplest details of everyday life. From these proceed the decision about the ultimate rightness and wrongness of everything, about good and evil in the widest sense. They again provide us with an answer to the question raised above. Revelation is the event in which God reveals Himself and at the same time the situation of the world. It is at once judgment and also grace and a new beginning. Our attitude towards it is decision pure and simple because of our power of genuine freedom. But the freedom disappears as soon as our dominion over the world is not in its proper place and proportion.

The purpose of life may be described as the realization of values. The word is not employed in an idealistic sense but to express the meaning of existence. "Value" is what makes a being worthy to exist and an action worth performing. The value attaches to the being itself as its essential and significant content; it also transcends it as the standard by which it

---

40. This idea is re-examined in connection with the problem of destiny. Cf. pp. 204ff.

is measured. Finally, "value" denotes the creative thought of God which establishes the essence and significance of the being. To speak of values is thus a shortened way of speaking about the particular character of being.

Every genuine value has its significance within itself. "Strength" is just strength and, because it is something primary, it cannot be derived from any other source. A man can realize it only out of itself by acting "strongly" and growing "strong." But the fact also remains that the man is essentially strong only when he is also just. Justice differs from strength, has its own significance, from which alone it can be put into practice. As soon as a man seeks power without justice, it is immediately altered. It becomes violence and brutality with a void of weakness inside it. Correspondingly, true justice preserves its character only when reinforced by courage, otherwise it may drift into insecurity and indecision. Utility again is utility and it indicates that an action is directed towards a rational purpose related to human existence. It becomes unfruitful, however, tiresome, and finally unreasonable unless it has also a relation to the spontaneous development of life, to pure zest in growth and the joyfulness of existence. Similarly, this group of values becomes frivolous, trivial, and wasteful if they drift from the order of intelligible ends. A careful analysis of wisdom would show that it requires to be related to the irrational and even to "folly" since otherwise it can be mere pedantry and lose touch with reality; that beauty can be superficial and destructive where it is not subject to a serious moral purpose; and that without the free flow of mercy justice changes into injustice, and so forth. Freedom consists in pure surrender to the value, but if this is not continually related to complementary values, it shuts itself up, as it were, and is made a prison.

Each value is a primary feature, established in itself. It is related also to other values and its character is preserved by this relationship. These values are themselves directed towards still further values so that we have a structure that makes itself felt in all activity. The Right, as an expression of what ought to be willed and done in the circumstances, is always complex and flexible. It is a balance that must constantly be readjusted to concrete reality if the whole structure is to avoid being hardened. The same is true of the various stages and levels of value within the universe. Animate being, for example, presupposes inanimate being. Man, in his biological capacity, rests everywhere upon the realm of inorganic existence. On the other hand, it is equally clear that the final conclusions of inanimate being are drawn only in the animate world. Mechanism, for instance, realizes its fuller possibilities in the organic world, which is essentially higher and different. Correspondingly, the spiritual factor has a continually changing relation to the vital element: an ethical attitude presupposes always biological potentialities. On the other hand, man's health, quite different from that of an animal, finds its last safeguard in the ethical order, to wit, man's responsibility for his existence. These glimpses suggest the vision of a whole, of a realm of values as the reflection of the significant content of the world, from which alone each value derives its truth. The question remains whether this realm of values can establish its unity from itself alone.

The world which finds its centre in man has its orientation towards God. A man with one of the keenest eyes for reality has said that "man infinitely transcends man."[41] Man soars above his own level and does not fully realize himself until he is in contact with God. In a certain sense this is also valid of the world. The self-sufficient world, postulated by some modern thinkers, does not exist, it was a postulate of revolt. What does exist is the world related to God through man. Man, therefore, in Augustine's memorable phrase, is by his very essence a searcher, and in man the world also is searching. The only realization of values which

41. Pascal, *Pensées*, Fragment 434.

leads to freedom includes this knowledge and recognition. Yet, unaided, this quest does not reach its goal because of the confusion in which it is enshrouded along with the human existence from which it proceeds. In consequence, it requires revelation and redemption and it discovers the way only in faith. Revelation, which proceeds from God's free will, shows the goal to which all values are directed and it therefore provides the final safeguard for human freedom.

Appendix: The Logical Problem of the Free Act

From what has been said about free action there arise some difficult logical problems. We cannot deal with them here one by one but we must at least point out the focus around which they accumulate, the problem of how the freedom which is claimed stands with regard to the law of causality.

The principle of causality declares that every effect has a sufficient cause for its occurrence and for its occurrence in this particular way. The experience just described (i.e., that of the free act) asserts that free action takes place because an inner initiative activates one definite possibility latent in the concrete situation but that this activation requires no cause outside itself to set it moving but is a genuine source, deriving from itself. Does this abrogate the axiom of causality? Is this an instance of an event without a sufficient cause?

Reply: That is so only if the axiom is interpreted in one particular way, namely, that the cause of an event must always lie outside the centre in which it occurs; in other words, that every event represents a universal process of transition. This would find concrete expression in things but only in the sense that they would provide the area and setting for the universal process. But my experience in reality is this, that the free act does not pass transitively through me but originates in me. The self-movement of spirit, the deciding will, is itself the cause.

Another objection: The alleged experience misrepresents the situation. Even that initiative which the subject imagines he finds within himself has causes which do not lie within him. Every action has a motive; it happens for some reason, and that precisely is its cause. Our experience of "freedom" merely indicates that the act of initiative is brought about not by mechanical or biological impulses but through intellectual and spiritual motives.

Reply: This objection assumes an interpretation of the principle of causality which cannot be justified. Certainly, free choice has its cause, and this causality rests upon the motive. But (all unnoticed) the objection slips the idea of "efficient cause" beneath that of "cause" and supposes the efficiency to proceed from the motive. If this were so, then the effect would necessarily follow and it could be deduced from the motives. This notion is contradicted by experience. Experience tells us that every free act, to be sure, has its motive; it occurs "for this or that reason." The existence of motives makes it a free and not an arbitrary act. It establishes the "reasonableness" of the action, the intelligible content directing the act of detachment and choice, as it has been described above. But the motive does not compel the act of initiative, it only provides it with a basis and gives it a meaning. The act as such proceeds from itself. If I ask why I go this way rather than that, the reply is that it is shorter and I shall arrive more quickly. To the further query, why do I want to arrive more rapidly, comes the answer that there is some important duty to be done when I arrive. Again, a motive, namely, the objective which I want directly to reach, and so forth. I can go further and further along this line since Being forms one total pattern in which each element is associated with neighbouring elements. There is, however, another question, not in this line of inquiry, to wit: Why do I allow the wish to move rapidly and the desire to arrive to be the decisive factors? Why do I put them into effect? The answer is: Because I want to. And it denotes pure initiative. Naturally, motives can be introduced as grounds, as for instance: I will do this because I want to fulfil my duty or because I am acting reasonably or just because I want to act, and so on. But this merely gives a slight displacement to the final "because I want to" that expresses the reality of initiative. Sooner or later it must come in. In fact, it is there all the time, in attendance on every conceivable motive. For it merely indicates the manner in which the motive, whatever it be, is realized by the power of initiative; and the permanent mark which keeps us aware of this realization is our consciousness of responsibility.

The context we have been analysing contains the essence of what is known as the "free" act. It is part of the existential order of being and values; it "has a significance" which is set forth in motives and reasons, in a man's replies to the question: Why are you doing that? But man realizes this significance not in a transitive process nor through any inner necessity, imposed on him by motives, but in a spontaneous initiative.

It is useless to inquire whether such a form of causality is possible: it actually exists. Recognition of the facts must come before discussion of the problem. In consequence, causality does operate in two ways, that of necessity and that of freedom. Causality is always there, the effect has its adequate basis, an answer can always be found for the question how the effect was produced.[42] But there is a variety in the manner in which causality is effected. It may be transitive necessity or it may also be an

42. This needs to be emphasized in view of a peculiar opinion met with in many quarters, and it is uncertain whether we must interpret it as imprecision of language or, worse even, as confusion of thought—namely, that the principle of causality is no longer without exceptions. But if it is not universally valid, then it is not "valid" at all, and we are left with chaos. The principle of causality is always and necessarily valid. It is disturbing to discover that a dogmatic Determinism, which repudiates the very evident reality of freedom, should be ready to abandon the principle of causality.

initiative deriving from itself for which there exist motives; it can, how-
78 ever, neither be compelled by them nor deduced from them but on the contrary has to be accepted by them.

It is in this acceptance of what proceeds from free initiative that is rooted our reverence for the human person. Necessity we can control; we can foretell and calculate what necessarily happens and enforce it through the due arrangement of its elements. But here, on the contrary, we have to respect and trust and accept. The world is so constituted that it contains these two kinds of process and these forms of reaction. This admission may be embarrassing, and men in fact are always doing what they can to rid themselves of this embarrassment: in theory, by denying freedom, in practice, by hindering men in its exercise and putting pressure, both physical and spiritual, on them. But this does not get rid of the reality of freedom, and from time to time it breaks out in disastrous crises for the lives of both individuals and societies.

But—it might be argued—does not this endanger the whole system of the world? Here we find betrayed one of the crucial reasons why freedom is repudiated. This is the attitude towards life that is never sure of itself unless everything happens in a compulsive and even calculable way. At its heart lies an uneasiness and, closely linked with it, the will to mastery or, more precisely, the will to power. Its consequence is the mechanistic view of the world in which free activity would be both unintelligible and impossible.

But the world is no mechanism, no rigid system of forces that work through it; it possesses everywhere centres from which freedom operates. Their act arising from itself does not disturb the universal order, which accepts the result of the free act into its total pattern. This universal order is in fact related to this kind of act and in it finds its own fulfilment. In other words, the world as Nature is orientated towards the world as history.

This clarifies a state of things which the Idealists try to circumvent. They do not deny freedom but they attempt so to interpret it that it does not interfere with necessity. Here they appeal to a general principle by which the spiritual, moral, and religious elements are removed from all contact with empirical, material reality. Idealism thus postulates two worlds: the first, that of Nature and of knowledge based on logic, in which there is nothing but necessity; the second, that of spirit, which includes freedom. These worlds are supposed to cross one another in what is postulated as a centre, whether of self or the Absolute. But this is quite untrue. A closer study of history will show the harm done by the theory that spirit is enclosed within its own sphere, be it that of inwardness or pure ideality, while reality—and in practice, this means power—is left to its own devices.

There is only one world. To be sure, it has various departments; and there are many variants upon its fundamental principles but all within the one world. It must, of course, be so envisaged that it can embrace reality entire. It cannot be understood from any partial principle, mechanically from inanimate nature or biologically from animate nature, but only as a whole. And if we come to the conclusion that there is no one universal principle, that is quite in order. The "world"—that is, the totality of existence—must in that case be too great for any one single principle.

Previously, we insisted that the world is not shattered or even disturbed through free activity but that it is capable of assuming it into itself. We might go further and suggest that the world has receptacles for and anticipations of freedom. A few of these may be set down here in question form.

Two are from the field of Nature itself:

Can we derive the emergence of biological species entirely from their predecessors? When a new species emerges, does this mean that

we discover efficient causes in its natural precedents and circumstances?
80 What does logic make of *mutation*, the sudden emergence, without efficient causality, of a new species out of living spontaneity?

If I understand the matter correctly, no reason can be given for the movement of a single atom in space. Absolute laws can be formulated for the movement of a mass of atoms but not for an individual atom. Hence the thesis that the behaviour of the atom is not "causal" but can be grasped only statistically. Could this perhaps indicate the logical if incomplete acceptance of the fact that we have here the beginning of a causal process which not only transposes but originates?

Two other phenomena come from natural philosophy:

Can the individuality of a single biological specimen—that is, not the typical structure nor the acquired characteristics but the individual character as such—be derived from parents, ancestors, environment, and such factors? The shape, bearing, movement, the particular qualities which allow a shepherd, for instance, to recognize unmistakably every one among hundreds of sheep of the same kind and breed?

Is "quality," as we term it, in any sense to be derived from causes that are outside it? Take the quality "red" in its full range: the vibration of light with its formula, the sensitive quality of the eye, the psychological content of experience, the intellectual meaning for the mind—can all this be derived from other sources or does it present us with a primary datum that simply has to be accepted? Is not the same valid for every real natural form, like those of the "rock crystal" and the "oak"?

There remains one last and fundamental reflection. Can finite Being as such, the world in its immense but still finite dimensions, its unspeakably rich but still characteristically determined nature—can finite Being be conceived as necessary? Certainly not. Only an infinite and absolute world could be necessary, in the sense that it is incapable of not existing. But no such world exists. What we have is the finite world, with such and such dimensions, with these and the other qualifications, a world constructed and set in motion. We cannot prove that this world had to exist, we can only learn from experience that it does exist. It cannot be deduced, it has to be accepted. Does this not already embrace the first design and anticipation of freedom in the genuine sense?

These items we have gathered together are surely linked one with another. Do they not suppose another form of causality different from necessary causation?

Grace

THE PROBLEM

The previous section traced the phenomenon of freedom through the different levels of existence. Eventually it merged into the phenomenon of grace, so that the concluding paragraphs dealt with grace as much as with freedom. In retrospect we can see that grace is not only a precondition of freedom in the new life, made possible through Redemption, but that, even apart from this, if freedom is to develop, a factor of a special sort is required which must be much akin to grace itself, as it were, a generosity of being that points to the generosity of the Creator.

The very form of the word shows that the idea is understood in an improper sense[1] *that calls for some explanation. Revelation has a special relation to immediate existence. Its communication to man comes from the pure generosity of God. It is not a higher level nor is it a deeper inwardness in the possibilities of this world; it differs from any this-worldly aspect that can be imagined. To employ a somewhat indefinite term, it is "supernatural." But*

1. Translator's Note: The words in the original text are *Gnade* and *gnadenartig*, that is *grace* and *resembling grace* or *akin to grace*. Later, the term *gnadenhaft* is employed to denote, as though by a parallel with supernatural grace, what Nature, art, or life gives us spontaneously and generously. It might be best translated as the "gracious."

the God of revelation is the same God who created the world and therefore the relation between revelation and the world is not merely one of difference. The Creator ordinated the world towards revelation, and this fundamental reality of existence has not been suppressed by sin. Scattered throughout the world are premonitions from which, in themselves, no single detail of revelation could be deduced but, once revelation has taken place, the Logos, as John declares, "without whom was made nothing that was made" comes "unto his own"; and created being remains His property, even though it has turned against Him in sin and "His own received Him not" (John 1:3–11). Thus a light is cast by revelation also on the things of the world. The paradox is in fact true that the real significance of these worldly things issues not from the things themselves but, in the first instance, from revelation. In other words, the reality and values of this world of our immediate experience are finally understood and made operative through the providence with which the Redemption has surrounded them.

The term "grace" has a precise meaning that must not be diluted if revelation is not to degenerate into a philosophy of doubtful worth. But it is nevertheless true that you can discover in the world anticipations, correspondences, and intimations that point towards grace in the more precise sense. Only positive revelation can disclose and develop them. We shall refer to them in these reflections as the "gracious."

We must first discover the point in the world at which this element of the "gracious" can be grasped most readily, then move to a number of factors less easy to comprehend, and in conclusion ask whether or not an element of this kind must necessarily be present. We shall then speak of grace in the proper meaning of the word. This will be clearly differentiated from all that has preceded it as something distinct and unique in its holiness, and we shall make use of and draw the final conclusions from elements in the world which God has related to it.

THE "GRACIOUS" AS AN ELEMENT OF IMMEDIATE EXISTENCE

The "Gracious" in Relation to Authority

The significance of "gracious" in its this-worldly sense is most clearly seen in the realm of law and the State. The "State" is the manner in which a people as such is capable of playing a rôle in history. Without some form of State organization, a people lacks form and capacity for action. The State is based upon two factors: an order determined by right and a concrete human authority. If the order be just, then it enjoys validity, but authority is needed to put it into effect. Authority is a matter of immediate fact but it requires to be justified by order.

The order in the State is prevailing right, the law. This must be made effective as soon as it is recognized as valid, and the responsibility for this fulfilment rests with the supreme authority, the head of the State—king or president according to the constitution or whatever constitutional form the office may assume. Its holder may, however, adopt another position. He can do something directly from his own full powers which is not contained in the law, for instance, grant a privilege or suspend a legal process which would normally be carried through, for example, a punishment. This is the act of grace which grants something which the recipient can neither claim of right nor compel through force. Its source is the free initiative of the supreme authority and its purpose is to create a realm of the abnormal above the juridical order to deal with unpredictable situations which do arise. This act of grace rises above the law and in the particular case suspends the law but it is foreseen by the law and in the last resort is its safeguard. For it makes clear that law is not part of the natural order, functioning on natural lines, but has reference to personal and free beings. As this disposition of grace can proceed only from the initiative of the supreme authority, so it can be accepted only through the freedom of his subject. An animal can no more be the recipient of mercy than a natural force can bestow it.

In a less noticeable form, this attitude of grace recurs in all relationships of authority, in that of parents to children, of superior to inferior, and so forth. These relationships are regulated by a "law," an order arising from the nature of the relation, but they leave room for free initiative by which the person wielding authority can adjust himself more fully to concrete circumstances that cannot be wholly dealt with in any system.

This relation of superior to inferior assumes a new note when it is based not on right but on fact, not on office and authority but on the force and significance of being, for instance, in the relation of stronger to weaker, wealthier to poorer, of those with greater vital resources or greater intellectual or moral qualities to such as are less gifted. Here too there is room for graciousness, for a generosity that gives and rescues. The situation is of course more complicated. Since Right is not there as a focus for action, there is a danger that the recipient of such graciousness may feel threatened thereby in his personal dignity. That is not so in a juridical system. The head of the State, the supreme authority, "grants graces"; he is a definite person but he is acting in virtue of that authority. The right to "grace" is the obverse and less familiar side of one and the same official authority whose other and more familiar side is concerned with preserving the standards of law. Thus the all too personal note is toned down and the dignity of the recipient of the "grace" is not infringed. It is different in the other instances that have been alleged. There you have no juridical order but a relation of superiority that introduces a problem for the inferior. If he acknowledges the superior's right to be "gracious," then the superior must banish any selfish reference from his attitude and desire to be merely a channel through which this splendid possibility of converting power into graciousness can be achieved. This is perhaps a definition of true courtesy.

The Creative: Inspiration and Achievement

The note of grace in what we have been examining was defined as the quality of action which can neither be compelled nor be claimed but arises from free initiative. This quality again recurs in the manner in which creative work and the creative act come into being. This provides us with a similar pair of opposites: creative activity is distinguished from its work as the act of grace from its legal consequences.

Work stems from reflection and effort, and within the limits of external circumstances and inner capacity it can be done at any time. The mark of creative work is different. It springs from inspiration and needs the favourable hour. You cannot reckon or force the flash of inspiration, the dawn of the idea or birth of the form, you cannot piece together the elements that will bring achievement or make a happy harmony of interior forces. The thing happens "in its own time" and it defies a utilitarian intention. This is not to imply that great works and acts of creation just happen. On the contrary, they presuppose incessant labour, great concentration, and much sacrifice. But all these can do is to prepare, assure, and develop the basis of all creation, which is inspiration. They cannot compel it. Nor can they compel the second factor, achievement—that combination of favourable circumstances which brings the hand that is fashioning into contact with the reality and makes fulfilment possible. This too cannot be forced. Calculation, influence, pressure may even hinder it. And then there is no room for the figure to emerge, the various elements to harmonize, and the balance to be achieved. True, there are methods to assist creative activity—sometimes of a queer sort—but these are effective only within narrow limits and then they are not without their danger. Think of the rôle played by stimulants and intoxicants in the lives of great artists or the way in which sleep can be made to subserve creativeness and, on the other hand, of the importance of signs, the constellations, and generally of "superstition" in the lives of creative personalities. In all of them may be found elements belonging to a creative technique. But fundamentally, the creative artist can only make the necessary preparations, put himself in a state of readiness, and for the rest pay the price that is demanded.

It is impossible to say where inspiration comes from. Normal work is a process proceeding from insight and resolution and it is carried on by a logical scheme of effort and perseverance. It can be so rationalized that it is indifferent who the workman is, to the last grade of depersonalization, at which the workman does nothing more than supervise the machine. Inspiration, on the other hand, springs from an original source that cannot be more closely determined. We are merely using words when we talk of individual creative centres which reach their peak point in the genius. A man senses that this centre is his innermost possession. In creating he has an intense feeling of being himself—a feeling that can soar upwards till it becomes exaggeration or even Hubris. When he creates something, he is *him-self* in the most concrete meaning of the word. On the other hand, he feels this original source as something outside his personality, above or beneath it, and as moving towards him to take possession of his self. It confronts his will with its own sovereign claims so forcibly that it may take away his initiative and frustrate his strongest desires. This sovereign character of inspiration is expressed, in classical imagery, as "genius." It is presumed to originate from the centre of the grand design of reality, and indeed the outlook of a great creative artist, a genius, has a character that can only be termed universal. When Dante or Shakespeare speaks, the universe itself seems to be in movement.[2]

2. A psychological interpretation of this is best sought in the theory of the unconscious. This refers to the hidden impulses and adaptations or submerged experiences from the individual past, the *subconscious*. There are in addition levels of personality connected with the group experience of family, nation, human nature, and finally the world itself, namely, the *unconscious* in the proper sense. As

So far as achievement is concerned, its final directing force is not in the creative artist but in the totality of Being. It involves a harmony of an immense number of elements, incapable of organization by the conscious will or the even more powerful and assured unconscious will. Among these factors are the favourable situation, the opportunity of the moment, and the historical framework. The intricacy and pressure of this force may be clearly seen if we reflect on the number of conditions, some of them quite unusual, which had to be harmonized to permit the production of the *Divina Commedia* or Shakespeare's dramas. The favourable moment wins a special note when it is wedded to a great achievement, the note of happy good fortune, in which power is curiously interblended with incalculability, and magic transmutation with the abiding risk of failure.[3] History tells us how strongly this sentiment has been experienced by active personalities. It takes us in the direction of destiny, which will be the subject of the next section.

It should again be observed that inspiration and achievement, the inward awakening and the favourable moment, do not necessarily coincide. It is wonderful when they do so and when conditions, both individual and general, are at the disposal of the creative work and act. But

---

a rule these elements are withdrawn from conscious thought and will, in greater or less degree, and their motives and forms rise up as though from a completely alien source. Nevertheless, they are individualized in the person in question, form a portion of his living substance, and so are found to belong to him. (Cf. C. G. Jung, "The Unconscious in the Normal and Pathological Mind," in *Two Essays on Analytical Psychology* [London and New York, 1929]. Reissued as "The Psychology of the Unconscious," in *Two Essays on Analytical Psychology* [London and New York, 1953]. The same theme is discussed in C. G. Jung and K. Kerényi, *Essays on a Science of Mythology* [New York, 1949].) The analysis of these factors may have some light to throw on the forms of creative fulfilment. But if we leave psychology to one side and put the simple question of the "What" and "How," we can discover little more than is contained in the figure of "genius" and the man possessing it.

3. Expressed in images like rolling dice, fragile glass, or unpredictable or blind Fortune.

the opposite may occur and you then have the tragedy of the unfortunate artist or hero.[4]

These instances reveal the "gracious" character of creation. It would be simplicity itself to suggest that in fact all this process is caused and develops in a continuous chain, and that therefore the impression of "grace" is an illusion, if not wholly meaningless. A world in which all movement is mechanically caused would have no more room for creation than it has for freedom; it would have room only for a necessary evolution of processes. But such a picture of the world is false and, in the final resort, unworthy. Mechanisms provide the world with a scaffolding, a system of functions to support it, but it contains another factor which is precisely the wellspring of genuine creation.

Encounter and Union

There is evidence of the same quality in the relations of men to one another. Each genuine I-Thou association comprises first the sum of what is contained in the two partners, but also another wider element, not produced by either or both of them but which appears as an original whole that gives significance to their association: friendship, partnership, love or, more exactly, this friendship, this partnership, this love. But this cannot happen unless a particular condition is fulfilled, namely, an *encounter*, and this too cannot be compelled.

One individual cannot create the other who belongs to him and who is to realize a full association with him. He cannot arrange to encounter the right person. To some extent he may seek for him but it is by no means certain that deliberate search makes an encounter more likely. It has its point when we are thinking of purposes, but not always even

4. The latter is presented very powerfully and without any psychological interpretation in the old Icelandic saga of strong Grettir (ed. P. Herrmann, 1913).

then, since on occasions we come across an achievement which presupposed a free rein for unconscious factors. Where it is wholly a matter of realizing a spiritual value, this deliberate search does positive harm for it narrows and hardens. What is paramount here is an attitude that blends indetermination with readiness. This is where reality makes its powerful appeal, very different from that of reckoning and planning. From this latter angle, a genuine encounter always appears to be "chance." A train is late and I don't meet the man; I made some mistake and this very mistake brought me into contact with him. This "chance" has its special mark, for as soon as it has operated, and the relation has been initiated, men feel that "it could not have happened otherwise," we "had" to meet, we were meant for one another, and this feeling may culminate in metaphysical notions like those described by Aristophanes in the *Symposium* of Plato, where he speaks of eternal human units, separated on earth into the two sexes and compelled to go searching, one for the other (193, c–d). Here again there is "grace." Something comes into being which cannot be claimed or calculated or compelled and yet it contains an undeniable significance. For one man or for many men it is indispensable for the full realization of life and yet it depends on the activity of a "centre" over which they have no direct control.

It is impossible to determine where this centre is. We can detect a convergent series of lines which point to one source but we cannot grasp the source. This touches on the problem of the pattern of destiny, which must be relegated to the following section. However, it is sufficiently evident that this "centre" cannot lie in individual existence or in a wider department of existence but must belong to Being as a whole, and that our view of its nature will depend on whether we accept or do not accept the existence of one single and intelligible purpose throughout Being.

Similar to this grace in encounter is that seen in a change of circumstances which brings release and help, when through some event, again not subject to calculation or compulsion, a pressing burden is lifted or a ray of light breaks in upon a situation of hopelessness or when life is assisted in some way. We have the impression of a grace because its causes lie outside the vision and capacity of the individual and yet effectively operate within his sphere of life. In this operation there is also a note of transcendence. It has an existential meaning which transcends the physical and psychical realms. It not only includes a factual change and betterment of the situation but in a more special measure it strengthens confidence in the providence of Being and intensifies the will to live.

Attention should be drawn to what is implied in the forms of grace we have been describing. Because these events and circumstances cannot be explained through the right or power of individuals, they point to an absolute and self-contained glory rising high above the horizon of empirical Being—the glory, namely, of God. The religious man becomes conscious of this whole orientation which is the fundamental factor in this phenomenon of grace. We shall deal with it separately. For the rest, it takes us over into the problem of destiny.

Euphoria and the Perfect

Another form of this graciousness is discovered in what may be called the moment of perfect peace. We understand it not as an occurrence but as a state, in which life is made aware of itself in its richness and perfection and as serene and free. A man feels that all is well; he has no unfulfilled desires; existence is complete. There has been no notable change in things or in the man himself but a balance has been achieved. The tensions which are part of life are not removed—that might bring boredom and satiety—but they have reached a harmony, full of meaning and yet delicately flexible, with the promise of an ultimate fulfilment.

This condition finds its symbol in the twilight of very clear days. Seen in it, objects seem to enjoy the full range of their essential form and at the same time they become transparent, letting us glimpse through them some ultimate and unique reality. A mysterious presence, to which we can give no name, radiates contentment. This mood is expressed with a beautiful sensitiveness in Hölderlin's poetry.[5] Nietzsche associates it with the silence of the noonday heat in a similar but slightly more questionable way. Psychologically, this condition is euphoria. In its normal range it signifies a culminating point and an inward serenity of life, a moment when this life is conscious of what it might achieve and aspire towards, before it sinks back into the confusion of the daily round. But it may also grow to alarming dimensions. States of high euphoria are closely associated with illness, and there can be no doubt that the descriptions of cosmic euphoria which we discover in *Zarathustra* and in many passages from Hölderlin's *Hymns* heralded the subsequent mental collapse.

The condition we have been analysing cannot be brought on through pressure. It is not to be confused with the peaceful harmony that comes from a healthy way of life or a long process of self-discipline. This is related to the moment of perfect peace as is planning to encounter, or work to creation, or a juridical process to the act of grace. It is true that you can encourage this euphoria deliberately as you can creative inspiration, at least to some extent. Means to this end have existed among all peoples and at all times: materially, alcoholic drinks or drugs that intoxicate or produce ecstasy; psychologically, through techniques inducing release or self-intensification. But such results are not genuine and the methods employed are dangerous. They make inroads upon that part of life which man should control and for which he bears responsibility: character, the quality of candour, order, honour, and loyalty. The true "moment of perfect peace" can spring only from itself, as favour and grace.

5. "The Rhine" (II, 12–13) and "At the Source of the Danube" (I, 2–3), pp. 207 and 167, in *Hölderlin: Poems,* trans. Michael Hamburger (New York, 1952).

It is as difficult to say whence it comes as it is to explain the source of the other forms of "gracious" process. Notions like those of a life centre or an interior proportion suggest themselves. It was no accident that Nietzsche with his wide experience of euphoria and its opposite state spoke in a mysterious tone of "mean and measure." The phrase may not explain but it does show the direction of this experience.

Closely linked with this impression of grace is that characteristic feeling, stirred from time to time by a perfect natural scene, by a natural scene whose proportions fit in harmoniously with our own personal feelings and do not swamp them with its immensity, sublimity, or depth. Such feeling does not arise when we contemplate a gigantic mountain or stormy sea but when we look at a perfectly lovely tree as in Mörike's poem on the "beautiful beech" or a noble animal, as in the early paintings of deer by Franz Marc. The gracious note here derives from the fact that such forms actually exist. Existence does not look kindly on the emergence of the perfect but in these cases it has "fortunately" happened. We are thereby affected in two ways: we see something rare and lovely, but also Being that was disintegrated is reintegrated once again at this particular point. There is a momentary peace amid the continual struggle and amid the weariness of the day's routine the hint of a bliss that may yet be attained.

There are some works of art that have the same quality: again, not the most powerful or sublime or the most profound but those that are purely graceful. It is not found in pictures of Matthias Grünewald or the sculptures of Michelangelo, but Mörike reveals it when he writes of the lamp hanging in the deserted room, and concludes with the supremely happy phrase that "*das Schöne*" (the beautiful) is what "*selig ist in ihm selbst*" (what is blessed in itself). Many a Greek vase has this distinction of sheer felicity and gracefulness, and also several paintings by Raphael and compositions of Mozart's. It takes force for granted and shows how it rises from its interior source to express itself in released loveliness and radiant happiness. This release of loveliness is the original meaning of the Greek word for grace, *charis*. The Italian *grazia* and the French *grâce* retain it.

In conclusion, it should be noted that there are men whose character is felt to be gracious. This quality is once again not associated with greatness, which, be it creative or dominant or of whatever kind, gives us a feeling of distance. The quality of grace consists rather in a proportion to ourselves; it contains something that serves to release and bring good fortune. Such men have an ease in their manner of speech and their approach to things. They prove that purity and nobility do exist in this world of confusion and violence. We recall Goethe's notion of the "beautiful soul." This impression may be intensified till it suggests something beyond this world. Contact with a man of this sort prompts the feeling that he comes from another world and brings a message with him to the effect that "they" have good intentions towards us and that they guarantee this message, despite the contradictions of day-to-day reality. Novalis appears to have been this kind of man. But here once more, proportion is necessary. No sooner is the impression intensified than the feeling of grace disappears, to be replaced by that of reverence or awe. This perhaps is the case of Hölderlin.

The Grace Element in Being

All that has been said points to the presence within Being of a factor with the mark of the gracious. Its meaning will be made clearer if we ask the question we previously asked about freedom: In what kind of world could this phenomenon not exist?

The answer is in a world constructed along the lines of mechanical science. If everything could be resolved into mathematical, biological, and psychological necessity then these phenomena would be impossible. Everything would have the mark of radical necessity and could be foreseen and calculated, even though the design might be highly complicated. It would be a world without grace. Nowhere would you have a favour bestowed, the emergence of a new being, the happy achievement of perfection, the free expression of a heart. But where the feeling for such moments of grace appeared, it would be either an illusion through lack of insight and judgment, or a constitutive illusion, needed by Nature to sustain the individual's powers and will to live. A man conscious of this would discover the real connections between things and be in a position to realize all his potentialities.

There are certain human atmospheres that smother and even stifle this natural graciousness. By "atmosphere" I refer to that complex fashioned of prevalent images, accepted values, and predominant forms, with their network of spontaneous sympathies and antipathies, hopes and fears, which is paramount in some types of men and women. Other atmospheres encourage this element of grace in Being. On the individual plane, for instance, a warmhearted and kindly man; on the social, groups with artistic interests; historically, great creative periods. In such surroundings originality and creativeness are held in esteem; there is a general air of sympathy and therefore they emphasize, sustain, and challenge one another. Other atmospheres depreciate, discourage, and enfeeble it: for example, those of Puritan fanaticism, authoritarian bureaucracy, canny calculation, and, most hopeless of them all, that of power seeking rationally to justify itself, that mechanized inhumanity which has come to the fore in our modern era. Freedom, generosity, elevation of heart, humour, original inspiration, and confident enterprise—all this is regarded as alien, unsympathetic, disturbing, and even dangerous. An uneasiness is operating beneath the surface and it feels itself threatened by this natural grace, which it attempts to stifle.

But the real world includes in addition to this co-ordinated interrelation an original source and all that derives from it: not only what is rational and transparent but an element also that is unpredictable and creative. Factors like this do not disturb the world; they help to construct it. They are the foundation of its potentiality, the possibility of a "new" element, which means not only that a thing has come into existence for the first time; it denotes a mark of Being which belongs to every genuinely interior gesture.

The same element recurs in the realm of human activities and destinies. We call it "disposition," the way in which events are related to personal existence, the manner in which they present and communicate themselves, even the way in which at times they enclose and refuse themselves, in disfavour. More will be said of this in the third section.

It is a fact that certain values in their proper realm—those associated with the noble and lofty—can be realized only where deliberate purpose is excluded. No planning or designing is of use here; they have to be given and accepted. Reality is not favourable to these values; when they manifest themselves, they do so in the form not of an "achievement" but of a "despite" or a "victory." And the victory belongs not to deliberation or strenuous effort but to a favour which naturally is not readily granted. Dante's Beatrice is a symbol reminding us that the noblest virtues appear only in the form of gracious charm. Her smile is the power that without effort achieves the most striking results.[6]

A proof that this factor is present in Being may be discovered in sensations which could not be explained otherwise—those, namely, of wonder and gratitude: in wonder which does not merely arise from the fact that we do not yet understand; in gratitude, which is more than mere contentment. These sensations do more than register a process; they correspond to one note of created being, to wit, that it does not

6. Cf. Guardini, *Unterscheidung des Christlichen*, in the section *Seinsordnung und Aufstiegsbewegung in Dantes Göttliche Komödie*, p. 445.

contain its explanation within itself. Whatever is necessary, rationally or mechanically, can be understood in itself, however immense its ramifications. Consequently, every merely rational event, every technical and industrial achievement, becomes "old" and indifferent after it has been realized, and there is no more foolish misuse of the word than to speak of the "wonders of technique." Technique and rational production are the direct opposite of wonder and do not occasion genuine astonishment or real gratitude.

The sentiment of good fortune adds another pointer in the same direction: once again, it is not the feeling of a need satisfied or of comfort but of genuine good fortune with the acknowledgement that more has been given than could have been claimed or grasped.

All this is closely linked with freedom. In the first place, ontologically: we are tempted to declare that this constitutes the freedom of Being. In experience like this its boundaries widen, its self-enclosure starts to open itself. To quote the happy phrase of Hölderlin, Being "*blüht*," or blossoms. A being that was purely mechanical would be imprisoned within itself. Secondly, from man's reaction to this experience: he must understand and desire freedom before he can grasp these instances. His eyes have to open, his heart to dilate, he must be capable of enjoying what here unfolds from its own resources. This comes from generosity, which gives free rein to Being, and from the humour that can recognize meaning even in what is peculiar and contradictory.

Fairy tales are an attempt to concentrate wholly on this element. They represent Being with grace and favour triumphant. That is why children, whose world is constructed on these lines, naturally understand them. There is a deeper sense in which they are true also for adults for they assure them of one element they easily forget. Ageing, in the bad as distinct from the good sense, means that this feeling for grace disappears and that sensitiveness is hardened. Fairy stories are an antidote to this complaint, provided there is still some sensitiveness left to appreciate them.

Grace in the Religious Sphere

This gracious note is strongly developed in religious experience, understood as before in the general sense. It is fundamental for the character of religious phenomena. The numinous or Divine can exercise its influence with great intensity and important consequences, but it always remains "on the further shore." Its region cannot be reached by a movement on the worldly plane; it is attained only "in transcendence." It has an initiative of its own that cannot be directly grasped, restrained, or compelled but which springs from itself. The Divine is active when and how "it will." What it grants or achieves is a concession of favour that cannot be forced, just as refusal, wrath, and evil action spring from the unapproachable roots of *dis-grace.*

Of this there exists direct religious experience. Basic forms of the religious act or of religious possession, such as wonder, shock, fear, petition, blessedness, gratitude, show that their contents cannot be evoked by any method at man's disposition but that they come from a freedom which reserves its right to grant them, that is, they have the character of the gracious. Certain religious feelings contain an explicit reference to this grace, for instance, the consciousness that we have not deserved something, the attitude of humility, the sense of a vocation, prayer for forgiveness and pardon, indeed every prayer that is couched in a religious form.

Rationalism and its derived modes of welfare and social formation continue their efforts to get rid of this religious element with its attitude of grace and favour and to construct reality on transparent principles of reason, psychology, and social order or at least to interpret it as a solemn liturgy that can be controlled in measure and influence to support more

basic factors. Our first comment on this is that with the introduction
100 of rationalism and technology the character of the religious element is destroyed. It can exist only in the form of grace. The attempt completely to exclude it confronts us with the question whether the religious element is an original phenomenon, that is, belonging to the nature of Being, or only a secondary aspect that could be dispensed with or perhaps refashioned. Human experience insists that it is the former and thus confirms the results of an unprejudiced theoretical analysis. If this is so, then the religious element cannot be suppressed. The attempt to suppress it can only lead to consequences similar to those of efforts to suppress what is essentially spiritual, to wit, psychical illness in the individual and the community. Recent history has taught us some frightening lessons on this matter, which are likely to be confirmed in the decades that lie ahead, for anyone with the intelligence and courage to understand them.

There is, however, one point on the religious plane which appears to contradict what we have been saying. Once a religion has become part of the life of a people and has created a tradition, a systematic pattern of life is brought into existence which imposes itself on its subjects. This obligation makes the believer feel that he has rights against the supreme religious power that has given the law or in whose name it has been promulgated. And so a restriction is set upon the initiative of the numen and the graciousness of his conduct is limited.

This notion of a claim in right is often accompanied by the idea of an extra force that can be exercised upon the numen. Its most conspicuous form is magic. This reposes on the assumption that the Divine attributes and power belong to the same total reality as the believer himself and are linked with him through a general law of association. Once man knows this law, he can exert pressure on the numen. Its simplest form is the knowledge of Divine names and their employment to put pressure on the deity, for incantation and the raising of spirits. More complicated examples are found in liturgical acts expressing a person's desire symbolically, with the belief that he can enforce its realization. These measures are intended to restrict the gracious element in God's relationship with man.

Halfway between the claim of Right and magical pressure is the manner in which asceticism and contemplation frequently attempt to exert their influence. Through a process of purification, detachment, and concentration the religious person advances to a state in which he stakes a claim against the numen because of God's delight in him or his likeness to the deity. In this condition of soul a man's religious powers may be so concentrated and heightened that the ascetic may actually feel he is exercising a force on the particular numen to which his service is directed.

These different attitudes affect an ever-widening area according as religious representations and beliefs are more and more debased. Indeed, they can so assume control as to destroy the proper character of religion and reduce the whole field of religion to a mere system of practical actions.

GRACE IN THE CHRISTIAN SENSE

The Creation of the World and Grace

We must now inquire into what revelation tells us concerning grace in order to form a proper concept. We start with one fact that might easily be overlooked.

Revelation teaches that God created the world out of nothing by His sovereign will. This implies that the world did not have to exist. That is confirmed by the sense of obligation which a man has—as one of his basic, existential experiences—of giving thanks for what he has and what happens to him, even for his existence and life or of protesting against what man is and even against his very existence. This gratitude and protest are not directed against this or the other happy or unhappy detail but against existence in itself.[7] Such reactions could not arise if the world were necessary. No amount of lyrical or pseudo-religious talk can obscure this. We can never give thanks for what has to happen and we can just as little protest against it, quite apart from the fact that we would be equally bound by the necessity. The whole of a man's perception and reaction would be part of the universal necessity: an attitude of gratitude or protest would be as unthinkable on his part as on that of an animal.

Once the world does exist, it includes necessity in its various forms but it is not necessary that the world itself, built out of these materials and forces, fashioned in accordance with these essential forms, and determined by these values, must actually exist. The forms of reality and value are necessary in what they signify, since they are the expression of God's eternal truth, but it is not necessary that the objects and relations in which they are realized should themselves exist. Their totality, the world, could have been constructed on other essential principles; it might even not exist. The opinion that the world must exist comes from definite existential attempts to make it an absolute. We find evidence of this very widespread at the present time and it has created the common notion of "Nature." By this is meant an ultimate something, behind which it is impossible to go and from which it is again impossible to appeal to a Higher Being. Everything thus coalesces in Nature and finds its meaning there. It is "Natural," that is to say, intelligible in itself, because established upon itself, sufficient for itself, and self-fulfilled. But this notion does not proceed from any true insight; it is a postulate that is at once an expression and an instrument of man's emancipation from God. In the

7. These feelings are brought out in great artistic figures, for instance, in Dostoyevsky's *Brothers Karamazov*, in the *staretz* Sossima, for whom creation is one long invitation to thanksgiving, and in Ivan Karamazov, who "refuses to accept it."

measure in which man can determine thought and, with thought, perception, revelation with its presentation of God and man, its significance and its language, becomes alien. In revelation the world is not "Nature" but creation, "work." It does not rest upon itself, it proceeds from the act of God. It is not therefore a necessary existent but something that has been done, a *fact*, a *Tat-sache* (an actual, factual thing).

This assertion of revelation differs completely from that described in myths, namely, that God fashioned the world out of a primeval chaos or that the world evolved from it under the direction of primeval forces. It declares that the world was called into being in the absolute and decisive sense of the word—wholly and in every part to its last material and spiritual foundations. This occurred not through an "It" or "Power" but through a "Someone," a "Personal Being," and the "Personal Being" *par excellence* who on His side is independent both of the world and of all previous necessity, the personal God. He is the "Lord" of Being, in that He is self-sufficient, free, and self-fulfilled. He is Lord also in His creation, since this is not conditioned through Being and thus once again necessary, proceeding, for example, from an urge to unfold His inner richness or showing the form in which He realizes Himself or the way in which He becomes self-aware, as has been asserted in various forms of pantheism from Plotinus to the later writings of Max Scheler. God's creation is in no way a function of His Being. It is not an "operation" but a "deed" and this deed is accomplished because God willed it so, that is, from absolute freedom. God would be Himself, fulfilled and self-sufficient, which means that everything would be fulfilled and self-sufficient, even if no world existed.

Consequently, the ultimate character of the world is not "Nature" but "History." Nature exists within the world, a reality constructed in accordance with certain principles without consciousness or liberty, which has to operate in conformity with these principles. But the world as a whole cannot be identified with this concept of Nature and just as little with the concept which Idealism has set up in opposition to Nature, that of a world spirit or consciousness in conflict with and at the same time dependent upon it. Such a spirit would be ultimately "Nature" all over again, though on a higher plane.[8]

It follows therefore that the world proceeds from "grace." Here we are employing the word in its theological meaning but still in a quite general way. The world is not necessarily what it is; it might have been different. It did not necessarily exist and might not have existed. It cannot consequently be derived from any presuppositions; it has to be accepted. The final choice lies between obedience and rebellion.

Nevertheless, the resolve to create is good. It is in effect love, as is made clearer in the course of revelation till it attains full clarity in the thought of Christ. God presents the world with its existence. God gives man, the individual in his concrete circumstances, and therefore myself, the gift of existence within the world. And this is good. The thought is continually emphasized in the account of creation. God sees and judges that the world is "good" and "very good" (Gen. 1:4–31).[9]

Only from this standpoint can God's relation to the world, as described in Genesis, be understood. The distinction between "grace" and "Nature" worked out in medieval and modern theology is found within that framework to which we have attributed the term "gracious." The

8. This modern concept of Nature as an all-pervading and self-sufficient totality seems to be on the wane. Experience compels men to the conclusion that Being is not at all "natural" but rather problematic and full of dangers and that man and the world are in a condition of continual crisis. This provides us with a new possibility of interpreting Scripture, that of understanding the world as God's instrument and man as God's responsible official. At the same time, this positive aspect suggests a new negative aspect, resulting in an even more radical rejection of God than was involved in the theory of the world as an absolute value.

9. The contradiction between this assertion and the actual situation of the world is the result of history, the history narrated in the third chapter of Genesis.

second and more specific meaning of grace must now be considered in greater detail.

Grace in Christian Existence

Man's situation differs from that of any other living being. Plants and animals are enclosed creatures, determined by their particular nature, and they develop and realize themselves from within as they also adapt themselves to the environment suitable for their nature. Man's position is otherwise. His situation is not natural, it is historical. It is the situation of a person. His existence is determined not by the necessity of a nature in process of realization but by freedom through which it can be fulfilled but could also be distorted and destroyed. Man's historical character denotes also that he comes into act not only from himself but also in an encounter with others.[10] "Encounter," however, is more than a simple relation to another thing: this applies to every living being in its network of continually altering adaptation to its environment, from which benefit as well as disadvantage accrues to it. It means that man comes into spiritual contact with things, that he knows and assesses them, adopts an attitude towards them and uses them, fashions them and creates with them. His capacities unfold and his personality expresses itself in the process, or, on the other hand, they may be restricted and destroyed.

By vision, knowledge, and judgment a man enters with life and being into the realm of meanings, comes under the influence of its high dignity, and is formed in the process. But all this can prove true or false, it may be constructive or destructive. The being of animals forms a simple whole with one focal point, Nature, that operates both in the animal and the things subordinated to it. Its approach to objects is conditioned by one clear and definite standard, the structure of the particular animal.

---

10. Cf. above, pp. 90ff.

In man, however, there exist two fundamental points: the man himself, with his individual spiritual being, and the external world. For him existence develops all the time from the interplay of these two elements, the latter of which, the object that confronts him, consists of factors over which he has but a limited control, and it includes what we know as destiny, luck, and chance, whereas the former is determined through freedom and can will or decline the encounter and realize it correctly or falsely. The whole of this process has the character of a compromise, a risk, and an uncertainty. This is brought out by the apparent paradox that man can find himself only when he abandons himself and passes across to the object confronting him; when he remains within himself and holds fast to himself, he loses himself.[11]

Encounters take place in the world in the most varied ways and they culminate in the great adventure of surrender to a man, an idea, a task. They are realized in the manifold relations of subordination and communion, friendship, love, exchange, and creation. The essential and final encounter, the encounter which is decisive for salvation, rises above the world to its creator, God. This is the object continually sought for in religious experience in general, but it cannot be realized adequately except where God Himself has made it possible.

God does this normally not by means of an interior movement of the individual but *historically*, by way of revelation. In this He made an approach to man, appealed to him, and received him into a new I-Thou relationship, in which man is enabled for the first time to rise to the stature which God intended for him, that of God's own image and likeness, His representative in the world, and a lord himself under the Divine Lordship. The whole process by which God has approached man with His free benevolence, spoken to him, raised him up to a special

---

11. On this matter, cf. Guardini, *Welt und Person*, pp. 107ff.

personal association with Himself, and given him a vitality proceeding from God's very life—all this is grace, in the proper sense.

This was first achieved in Paradise—a concept that needs to be freed from certain shallow and unreal interpretations of recent date. Paradise is not the natural situation of man before he had awakened to spiritual awareness, and it is no projection of a child's mentality into the mythical "long ago and far away." It was an existence which rose from the fact that man stood in full and undisturbed contact with God. At the same time, this existence was put to the test. It had to be decided whether man would affirm and preserve this sacred association or deny and destroy it. Revelation tells us that the latter occurred, not through any intrinsically necessary passage from natural innocence to sophisticated guilt but because of disobedience to the Lord of the world.[12] Man consequently fell from grace, and this apostasy went deep down into his innermost life. What was left was not the simple, natural man, sound in himself and fulfilled in his nature, wanting only a special association with God. Because God's ultimate design for man was achieved only in his encounter with God, man fell below the level of pure Nature and became the complex creature that we discover today, a complex creature embraced by no single category, himself out of order and creating further disorder, in revolt against God and in contradiction with himself.

12. The theory of an all-sufficient Nature includes the belief that evil is a necessary element in the whole natural complex, whether it is to be formulated as the will to knowledge, the break-through of self-consciousness, or in some other way. This makes Good and Evil merely relative and abolishes the meaning of ethics. Evil in fact is ultimately what *ought-not-to-be*, and ethical life is rooted in the affirmation of Good and the rejection of Evil. What is worth doing can be done from the standpoint of Good. In the last resort, Evil is what is absolutely superfluous and basically to be avoided. But this applies to man in the fullest sense only before the first sin, when everything lay open to him from the standpoint of Good. Sin disorganized existence, and man finds himself again and again in situations from which there is no escape.

From that moment man shouldered the weight of history. Had he been abandoned to himself, this would have been disastrous and desperate, at once the consequence of and expiation for sin. Revelation tells us, however, that God turned towards the world a second time and addressed Himself once again to man. This occurred in the history of salvation, which reached its culmination in Christ.

Through Christ God enters personally into history. Christ takes upon Himself man's guilt and destiny. Himself pure and holy, He experienced these Himself. He made expiation for them through suffering, which is in fact the essence of this experience, but also through an external fate that grew out of His inner disposition, His Being and activity. In Christ God encounters man, invites him to cross over to Him, and gives him what is a precondition for making that passage. If man listens to God, an association of a novel sort comes into being. God pardons the man his guilt, reveals His hidden truth, assures him of His loving good will, and creates in him the beginning of a new life which develops in existence upon earth and one day will be fully manifested. This is grace in the Christian sense.

Its more exact significance cannot be summed up in a few words. To begin with, it is God's mercy as this is revealed in Christ, His attitude towards man, His love. This love is not based upon anything in man that renders him worthy of the Divine love, since he is God's creature and owes to God both his nature and his existence. Its motive lies within itself; it is a free initiative, which wholly anticipates the being and rights of the object that it concerns. The love of God is a creative love and it establishes man in significance and existence.

Not that man in himself has no being or value, as has been suggested by a radical school of theological thought. This tries to safeguard God's honour by cutting man out altogether, as it were, and making the Divine love itself the object of God's love. But the true meaning of creation is precisely that created man exists only because of God but at the same time really exists, established in genuine reality and with a genuine significance. This is the man whom God loves. How this is possible is a mystery but no absurdity. If God loves man, He does so in conformity with God's truth. The account of creation informs us that after man was created "God saw all the things that He had made, and they were very good" (Gen. 1:31): "very good" not in their own right but because of God—and really so and in God's eyes, who judges absolutely. He has given to man such a mode of being that the Divine love for man conforms to Divine truth. The whole of the process by which God has this intention, required for this kind of action; by which He decides to create a finite being that can be the object of Divine love; and by which He loves this being in reality and truth and with a Divine earnestness—all this is grace, a pure decision of Divine bounty, which no external force can compel and no external right can claim.

This is beyond our power to conceive, even more so when God directs His love towards man, after man has rebelled against Him; this love is then a redeeming love. Under these altered circumstances we insist again that God's love for man cannot be based upon any intrinsic value in man because value, like being, is first conferred on man by God's creative love. Still less, more decidedly "less," can man's own being and action establish a claim upon God's love, once he has disrupted this relation of encounter and lost grace. God's decision to continue to love the rebel in a new way was an initiative of Divine freedom at a deeper level, a redeeming love. And this in its turn is a mystery but in no sense an absurdity, and in God's eyes this love for man is even more intelligible when it is a redeeming love.[13]

13. When the mind attempts to study this relation, which is so fundamental for Christian life, it finds itself peculiarly situated. It starts with one statement but soon realizes that this line of thought will lead to error. It is then drawn towards the

Grace is further the relationship to which God elevates man. God
110 approaches man, gives Himself to man, and enables man to receive Him. God calls man but also "draws" him so that he can approach Him (John 6:44). Man goes across from himself to God but in the process he discovers *himself.* He resigns himself to God and this resignation enables him for the first time to enter into full possession of himself. Grace is this manner of existence founded on this relationship. It signifies a share in God but it is God who has made that share possible.[14] It denotes a continuing reception of Divine love through which the real self develops.

Grace, finally, is everything operated by the relation we have been describing: enlightenment of mind, the ordering and strengthening of the will in good action, the interior life of love and familiar intercourse with God, the sanctification of life—in short, the rebirth to that new manhood of which Paul in particular has spoken so frequently and with such emphasis.[15]

John records a sentence of his Master in which this emerges very impressively. We have referred to it previously. It occurs in the conversation of Jesus with the Samaritan woman at Jacob's well: "He that shall drink of the water I will give him shall not thirst for ever. But the water that I will give him shall become in him a fountain of water, springing up into life everlasting" (John 4:13–14).[16] In this context grace is "life

---

contrary statement only to have the same experience there also. The first statement points continually to the second, and the only way of keeping near to the truth is to enclose both statements in a dialectical process of Christian existence such as is found, masterfully worked out, in the introductory chapters of St. Augustine's *Confessions*; cf. Guardini, *Anfang, eine Interpretation der ersten fünf Kapitel von Augustinus' Bekenntnissen* (1943).

14. Guardini, *Welt und Person*, pp. 20ff.
15. This is not a theological treatise and we do not therefore raise individual questions from the tractates on grace.
16. I owe this interpretation of the passage and the better understanding of grace it has given me to a conversation with Heinrich Kahlefeld.

everlasting," symbolized by water flowing from its Divine source and assuaging man's vital thirst, his yearning for that true and genuine Being intended by God and which God alone can confer. But how is this water given and drunk and possessed? Not because the sacred hand offers us a goblet or, we may say since the images become a trifle blurred, not that it brings the Divine stream to us so that in our thirst we drink from it. The water springing from the Divine source is given and thereupon it springs up as a source within the man who is drinking. It remains a gift and can only be possessed as something given, it is always received and for that very reason becomes an original source within the man who receives it, proper and appropriate to him. In Galatians Paul expresses this association in terms of Christ when he says: "I live, now not I, but Christ liveth in me" (2:20). Christ lives in me but this presence does not forcibly expel my self or replace it with His but, because He dwells within me, I attain to the essential fulness of my own life as designed by the creator.

Grace is at once that which just cannot be taken for granted and yet provides the last fulfilment. No human power can compel it, no human right lay claim to it: it is a pure decision of God's sovereign freedom. But in it God draws near to man so that man through this encounter may develop into the being which God would have him be. The full notion of grace includes both these elements. It is firstly pure favour and gift and then through it man becomes himself in the sense intended by God. As soon as either of these constitutive factors vanishes, the whole pattern collapses. For grace is no adventitious thing, the presence or absence of which leaves the essential character of man's life undisturbed. On the contrary, it is only by means of grace that man becomes what according to the Divine will he ought to be. On the other hand, grace is not a condition of his immediate human nature, it springs from the complete liberty of God. These statements involve no contradiction but an antinomy, the basic principle by which God has established human nature;

they provide a mystery, certainly, but no absurdity. We have discovered this only through revelation and only faith makes us certain of it. But if a man has a sound good will he comes to experience its truth.[17]

The analogy with personal love may help us to understand this. The lover knows that he cannot compel the love of the beloved but that it must come from the innermost liberty of the heart; yet his whole being depends upon that love. He realizes that he receives his last fulfilment from another but it is his own self which comes to itself, and his innermost being is thus realized. The intellect cannot dissect the structure of these relationships but the heart knows that it is so and most rightly so. There is a resemblance as well as a difference between this and grace. The relation of one human being to another is based on the human nature they share in common and the antinomy can be resolved in an association that requires nothing more to make it complete. God, on the other hand, stands in the freedom of His absolute sovereignty. Thus the

17. I trust that no accusation can be brought against this exposition on the grounds that it makes grace an essential element in man. Grace is "supernatural," transcending all the power and every claim of man. But when we use the term "man" to indicate that Being which God ultimately intended when He created him, it is evident that this can be realized only through grace. God did not design man as a "natural" being to fulfil his purpose, as do animals, within his natural environment. There is no such thing as the "natural" man. This is an abstraction which the theologian needs to draw certain distinctions and establish relationships. The only real man that exists is the man called to the order of grace. Either he obeys and is then raised above the merely natural level or he refuses obedience and falls below the level of Nature into a debasing dependence on evil. "Pure Nature" when applied to man is an imaginary yardstick by which he cannot measure himself. Modern Naturalism attempts to construct a purely natural man with a self-contained reality and significance. His only function is that of developing his natural capacities and his association with the world. Should he so please, he may enter also into a religious association but this is of no primary importance for his evolution because his manhood is wholly realized in the interplay of his own nature and that of the world. A little attention will show this theory to be false and that man's whole being is in a state of confusion that would be impossible if there existed a "natural man." It is therefore not a question of knowledge but a postulate of the will in order to emancipate itself from God.

relation of man to God is a relation to Pure Transcendence. But God has revealed that this relation does exist and His words contain a pledge, the like of which no man can give to his fellow men. God, who transcends all power and every claim, makes Himself present in a way in which no man can be present to his fellow men.

The Relation of Grace, Properly So Called, to "Graciousness" as an Element in the World

The problem now arises about the relation of grace in the strict sense and the element of "graciousness" in the world. We propose to discuss it as we did the relation of Christian to immediate freedom, in a series of unsystematized thoughts and suggestions.

It must first be said that grace differs essentially from the various elements of redemption and fulfilment, of encounter and failure that were considered earlier in this chapter. We were then dealing with phenomena of psychological and cultural life that are clearly differentiated from religious elements in the general sense and still more from the content of revelation. A sensitiveness to the grandeur and beauty of Nature or the possession of "art and knowledge" no more includes "religion" than a capacity for logic makes a moral personality.

How then are we to speak of those natural religious experiences of "graciousness" described earlier in this section?

They too represent something other than grace in the stricter sense, quite apart from the fact, already noted, that they are frequently confused and corrupted. We have accordingly to distinguish them with great caution, particularly in view of the danger from the modern Relativist standpoint that Christian ideas may be put on the same plane as these general religious notions and so dragged down to a this-worldly level. A Christian might well decide to leave them alone and to concentrate upon faith.

However, in their true character, they do point to the "invisible
114 being" of God which "from the creation of the world is clearly seen in His works and through the Spirit, namely, His eternal power and His divinity" (Rom. 1:19–20). They can therefore be purified and accepted into the Christian scheme of doctrine and life. Indeed, this must be done for otherwise they would be left hanging in empty space. To speak a little familiarly, there is no such thing as a chemically pure Christianity but only a living Christianity, realized by concrete man in a concrete world, which includes the experience of its creation by God and the operation within it of Divine Providence. Christmas, for instance, should bring the believer "the goodness and kindness of God our Saviour" (Tit. 3:4). But in the Christian celebration there is a hint of mankind's old sense of the mystery of the sun, as it sinks to its lowest point and seems to be threatened with total submersion, which, however, battles its way through and begins once again its salutary course. And quite properly so because—to adopt the style of John—Christ declares at Christmastide: "I am the true sun. What the visible sun is in image and symbol, that am I in reality and truth." These natural intimations may come to the surface in Christian experiences of grace and we then have a new creation fashioned out of the old material.

This can be applied to all those experiences and representations that lie at the basis of the great religions outside the Bible. They contain elements of truth valid prior to revelation. For the world even in its fallen condition belongs to God, and every truth, even though it be made to serve a false interpretation, is a spark from the Divine light. Besides, God remains free to direct an appeal of grace to man, wherever and whenever He may choose, and therefore we cannot judge whether or in what way He is active within the framework of a non-Biblical religion. None the less, the discipline of Zeus-worship or the principles of Buddhist asceticism or the contents of Chinese mysticism differ essentially from grace as this is understood in the Bible. To make precise distinctions calls frequently for a very close examination but this is a good deal more fruitful than modern Relativists care to concede now they have become so dogmatic; but in the last resort no pure worldly standpoint is enough. The ultimate point of reference is the Person of Christ. What is in contradiction to Him, what does not lead to Him, directly or indirectly, whatever is enclosed irrevocably in the world, however strong the sentiment of liberation, purification, and elevation of spirit it may arouse—all this cannot be from God.[18]

Now, can the particular character of grace and therefore its distinction from the general religious phenomena of "graciousness" be immediately experienced and assessed?

To start with, we must again insist that grace derives from the freedom of the Holy God and is directed towards a human being, whose capacities and interior harmony are confused and corrupted. It is thus doubtful whether a man can appeal to experience in dealing with grace. Basically, we have to wait for it in faith and man cannot control its operations. It can operate and leave behind no awareness of liberation or elevation. Decisive turning points in an individual's salvation may occur and he may remain completely unaware. There are periods for every believer when, sustained by an "imperceptibly fine" conscience, he has to persevere in sheer fidelity and pure obedience. On the other hand, experiences of God's presence, love, and goodness are of high importance for religious life and the believer should safeguard and make use of them. But masters of the spiritual life warn us against attaching too great

18. This sentence is forthright and it is not difficult for the sceptic and relativist to see in it "the intolerance of dogmatic religion." But where revelation in the proper sense is accepted and not merely a religious interpretation of life and where you have a universal and peremptory call of a personal God and not just fluctuating religious experience, it is the only attitude that can be adopted.

significance to them. Firstly, because they can be deceptive and considerable maturity is required at times to pass a sure judgment on them. The chief reason, however, is that if a believer fixes his attention too closely on them, he will be diverted from what is the essential. Christian life must have its orientation towards the living God who rules in grace. What makes us certain of Him is our confidence in Christ's Person and teaching. To live as a Christian means to live by faith and in obedience. In the last resort, it does not matter whether we have a sensitive experience of grace, whether we enjoy a sense of God's nearness and loving guidance or live in the arid darkness of pure fidelity.

This does not, however, rule out the possibility of genuine and trustworthy experience of God's administration of grace. For it is the actual man who is called to this association in grace, the concrete man with spirit and body, temperament and all his capacities, the man in himself and in his association with the world. As God has entrusted the meaning of His sacred truth to the logical and grammatical framework of human language so that His message may be announced in human speech and received by the human understanding, so he can also permit men to have living evidence that He draws near to the believer, comes into association with him and attracts him, and enlightens, strengthens, and directs him, and Scripture very frequently refers to a perception of Divine favour, goodness, love, and guidance. Every experience contains in itself a possibility of judgment and in his First Epistle to the Corinthians Paul speaks explicitly of a Christian's ability to differentiate between what really comes from God and what proceeds from the doubtful "numinosity" of the world. The standard that he places in his hand is the relation of the particular "spirit" to Christ. "You know that, when you were heathens, you went to dumb idols according as you were led. Wherefore, I give you to understand that no man speaking by the Spirit of God saith Anathema to Jesus. And no man can say the Lord Jesus, but by the Holy Spirit"

(1 Cor. 12:2–3). John speaks in the same strain. "Dearly beloved, believe not every spirit; but try the spirits if they be of God; because many false prophets are gone out into the world. By this is the spirit of God known. Every spirit which confesseth that Jesus Christ is come in the flesh is of God" (1 John 4:1–2).

Once grace in its proper sense has been distinguished from this-worldly phenomena of self-unfolding and communication, creation and happy chance, encounter and inspiration, in a word, from "graciousness" as an element in existence, there remains the question whether it could also have a positive relation to them. The question concerns the possibility of a Christian culture.

A Christian culture is possible for the simple reason that it has actually existed. During the Middle Ages there developed a cultural structure of impressive beauty. When it collapsed it was succeeded by another culture that broke away with increasing deliberation from revelation, though the Christian link has not yet been entirely severed. The last great culture style of the West, the Baroque, stands essentially within the Christian tradition. Even the late nineteenth century includes masterpieces like Bruckner's music that are completely permeated with Christian faith. What possibilities the future may bring we cannot foretell, but more precise analysis shows that these Christian attitudes and relationships are still operative on a wide scale in Western culture even where it may reject Christianity.

It has been objected recently that this whole cultural tradition had only an extrinsic relation to Christianity, that it manifested itself through Christian material and ideas because no others were in existence but that its spirit and significance were not Christian at all. This objection, as is evident, springs partly from a fixed philosophical position and in part from motives of propaganda. If we study the matter conscientiously, it becomes impossible to talk about a pagan character of the Middle Ages and the Baroque period. They are rooted in the very heart of the faith; their structures are built up from revealed truth and with the force of a believing mind and heart. Of course, they were established in the new historical situation which brought the Germanic tribes into contact with antiquity in its decline. It was the new humanity resulting from this association that lived and worked in it with that unique blend of inwardness and adventure, freshness and solemnity. This pattern of life and creation was permeated through and through by Christian revelation. Impossible to conceive the medieval State without belief in the overrule of the God of revelation, sovereign above the world, who had freed man for the dignity of Redemption and also attached him to Himself at the deepest level of his being. The figure of man presented in this culture presupposes the religious sentiments of the *Imitation of Christ*, its discipline of self-examination and its affective school of love, through which elements in man's personality are stirred to action which otherwise would have lain untouched. Medieval art came into being because the centuries-long experience of Redemption and man's new relation with God that resulted from it brought an immense awareness of existence, a firmness of character, and both force and delicacy of feeling which could not have developed in any other way. Relations between the sexes were steeped in Christian ideas of marriage and virginity. The pattern of medieval existence, with its proportions and its humanity, its realm of values and modes of expression, continually shows the influence exercised by the saints through their knowledge and freedom, their powerful guidance, and the influence of their lives. Much more could be said on this vast subject.

All these are ways in which grace acts upon a man's creative faculties, stirring and liberating them, purifying them, and setting them in due order. For what concerns the Christian demands of renunciation and self-conquest—that is, asceticism in the broadest sense—it took the bourgeois narrowness of recent years to miss its meaning. It is the price that was paid for that constant ascent from constraint to liberty, from this world of immediate experience into the region of the Divine, that was expressed in the works of medieval culture.

Let us now repeat the question, this time at its most sensitive point: What is the relation of revelation and faith to that peak point reached in the natural element of "graciousness," namely, creative genius?

The atmosphere of mystery and remoteness that gathers around genius comes from the fact that its inspiration and expression are not taken from the immediate body-soul complex but proceed from more remote regions of reality. The greater the work, the stronger is the impression that it transcends the being of the artist and that the world itself is speaking through it. The creative quality supposes a uniquely receptive attitude to the whole of Being. The creative artist must unfold himself and become an instrument or channel. In the process the points that normally fix a person's stability and quality become relaxed and widened. The pattern of his soul, if we may use the expression, has a sector that is open to Being as a whole; his individual focus is less concentrated than it is in uncreative persons, there are times when it seems to be dissolved altogether. The focus that attaches another person to itself and is attached to that other person is vaguer and weaker and at times appears to vanish. The capacity for personal association with others is endangered, and we see tragic instances of this in the marriages, friendships, and partnerships of creative artists. The same holds true for relations to self, loyalty to self, and responsibility. Inspiration releases a man to some extent from contact with reality; it intensifies his self-awareness; it induces him to confuse his real self and its concrete associations with his imaginative self and its productions. In the mind of pathological and creative men—this points to the greatest danger in creative expression—a feeling can grow that they have power over the world and could shake reality itself with their concepts: a confusion of finite with infinite creation resulting in a radical falsity and overweening violence. After inspiration has passed and the work has found external expression a reaction sets in. Characteristic depressions break out that are the antithesis to creative excitation. The artist has poured himself into his production, he feels that he is now nothing and is in danger of abandoning himself altogether or giving in to instincts and impulses. His personality is threatened from both sides, and it will preserve a balance only if safeguarded by moderation and self-esteem.[19] These dangers are also manifested in the characteristic mistrust which the creative artist arouses in persons whose lives are directed by utilitarian principles or are based on a sense of moral responsibility and real control of circumstances. There is something in creative natures which makes more ordinary people say that they value the work but not the artist.[20]

Human love can protect the creative artist to a certain extent but it cannot help in that final and most intimate relation which exists between genius and the being of the world. The only effective safeguard is provided by revelation, that is, grace in its strictest meaning. For this shows him what is above all human creation and it prevents him from confusing himself with God.[21] It ensures that his creation will never become the be-all and the end-all, that it is a purely cultural awareness. As long

---

19. Human beauty provides a characteristic parallel with this creative genius. Possibly it is in reality what creativeness is in achievement. It too cannot be deserved or compelled but only received as a favour. And, like creativeness, it involves a personal revelation of Being, at once a potentiality and a danger.
20. The highest degree of this—enthusiasm, rapture, and transformation—is found in the cult of Dionysus. Those who sing its praises usually ignore other intrinsic elements in it that are unreliable and disloyal, disintegrated and disintegrating, unworthy and debasing.
21. Properly speaking, no Christian ought to apply the term "creation" to man, for this usage threatens to obliterate the distinction between what God did, when He established the world with its reality and significance, and what man does, when he fashions this-worldly reality according to his will and expresses an interior vision in its material. But this use of the word has come to be accepted and we cannot do without it. Revelation will help us not to misunderstand it.

as man remains in the radiance of grace, the "graciousness" of creation is anchored in the truth. Its emotional content may perhaps be lessened. Medieval man did not throw himself into creative activity, making it a matter of life and death, as did Renaissance man. The latter's cultural activity was so intense not merely because he was highly gifted and the historical situation contained a unique store of opportunities. There was another, more hidden reason, namely, that he committed himself to this activity in a way that would not have occurred to the medieval man. In his eyes nothing stood above such creative work. Our present situation might be greatly eased if we could determine what decisive factor was lost and destroyed in those critical years of Western history. A superficial view sees in them only the break-through of freedom and the richness of culture but there remains the query whether something then drifted away and was left without helm or rudder. When one portion of man's being loses its bearings and drifts helplessly, the dark power that is always on the watch beneath—it will be treated later[22]—can force its way in and use the energies of this portion to imprison man within the world. Is this what then occurred? Did a demonic element then enter into the attitude of Western man? If this applies to creative artists it is correspondingly true of the men who appreciate the work and make it their own. It requires much courage to realize the extent to which modern man has idolized creative work and the unconditional, almost religious manner in which he has accepted "culture"[23] as the content of his existence.

22. Cf., in the third section, pp. 139ff., 148ff.

23. Cf. Guardini, *Welt und Person*, pp. 1ff. This idolization of culture paved the way for the twelve years of Nazi barbarism—the penalty for its false dialectic. What prevents man from sliding into the abyss is not something higher but something unconditional. If he refuses obedience to God in order to leave himself untrammelled for his great work, it is no longer possible to see what standards can still bind him. What is to prevent him from losing respect for high quality and in its place turning out facile and inferior productions?

Revelation and the principles of order that derive from it, that is,
122 grace in the proper sense, give man stability. The sentence, "What doth it profit a man if he gain the whole world and suffer the loss of his own soul?" (Matt. 16:26) penetrates more deeply than might at first sight appear. It involves a protection "of life" on all sides. In so far as it exalts a saintly life and eternal life above creative work, it shatters the absolute claim of the creative impulse, puts it in truth and in its own true proportion, and rescues it from the demonic element that endangers it.[24] A man who believes will never so completely lose the sense of his own being and run the risk of abandoning himself altogether, even in periods of inner emptiness, as a man left alone with himself and the world. What previously prevented him from falling a victim to creative intoxication now protects him from the demon of the void and prevents him from being overcome by formidable impulses.

It may be objected that the creative artist has to venture into all kinds of dangerous situations and experience exaggeration and deceit, privation and passion, if his work is to have its full intensity. Christian revelation, however, raises a firm protest against this sentiment, part of the modern worship of creativeness. No work can compensate for violent Hubris and the rejection of moral values. Works for which this price is paid are rotten at the core and would have been better left untouched. One of these modern tenets is that error, revolt, and evil are necessary for a work of greatness to be achieved. The tenet rests upon an interpretation of original sin as the desire for knowledge. According to this, mature knowledge, and, let us add, power of judgment, realization of values, and adult creative existence—all these were originally excluded. Being good would have been the equivalent of being ignorant, childish, and unfruitful. The man who would not accept such conditions had no

24. For the problem of work, cf. the Excursus at the end of this section, pp. 124ff.

alternative but to rebel and commit evil. This was how culture began and it has always retained its Promethean and godless character. The theory is abysmally false. It perpetuates Satan's original lie and calumniates God (Gen. 3:4–5). We have to put the question where it really belongs: prior to the fall, when man's nature was intact and unconfused. This man would have had no need of evil to fulfil the purpose of his own being, to achieve the good, just as he would not have required error to discover truth. On the contrary, truth, as in the old proverb, is "judge of itself and of falsity," and good is what "reveals itself and evil." Knowledge was intended to be won, and with it all that is implied in mature personality and rich work, but in obedience to the creator of the world. But man committed evil and fell into error and he now attempts to claim that this was necessary. Since man took his first decision to sin and since sin has become a power and created Being is damaged and entangled to its very roots, we discover continually that a good element is associated with the bad or that good is achieved by means of evil. Yet this is out of order and ought not to be. Man should make efforts to prevent this from happening, should struggle and make sacrifices for this. But when, instead of this, he converts this tragic confusion into a fundamental principle of his thinking, then he is reiterating the tempter's original lie.

Revelation puts things in their due alignment. It declares that whatever is worth attainment can be reached by way of truth but what has to be purchased with falsity and evil is not worth the realization, judged by eternal standards, which are the only proper standards. This may sound narrowminded but it is true. It is a writer's own fault if he is incapable of showing that truth shines more brightly and goodness blooms in more lively colours than their opposites.

Excursus: Work

124 The same is true of work. Modern man, and the German in particular, has long since lost the right approach to it and can no longer view it as part of a larger whole. It also has become demonic.

Its true meaning is defined in the words of the account of creation (Gen. 1:26–29; 2:8–9, 15–17)· The Divine image and likeness in man consists in man's power of dominion over the world, since God is the absolute Lord. "Work" is the sum total of those activities of cultivation, administration, and formation by which man exercises this dominion. But this retains its meaning only if the man who exercises them is subject to the Supreme Lord. At the moment when, deceived by Satan, he repudiates his obedience to God and determines to become master of his own graces, he loses control of that dominion and is made its prisoner. The dominion is changed into a demon who turns its former master into a slave and holds him prisoner within the world. God now gives work its second significance: it becomes punishment and penance (Gen. 3:17–19). With this God opens before man a new possibility, that of returning to his right association with God and himself by means of work. However, the measure in which man loses his grip upon faith is also the measure of his irrevocable enslavement to the demonic spirit.

This new attitude towards work has a long history behind it. The man of classical antiquity rejected work entirely and left it to slaves; he engaged in politics, conducted war, and lived for and enjoyed culture. The ground was not merely because work was arduous and humiliating—political and military life have their burden and humiliation—but because man in antiquity lacked the will to dominate the world in the manner that only work can make possible. His dominion was not in the economic and technical order but military and political.

Then a fundamental change sets in. Christianity abolishes, at first in theory, then gradually also in practice, the distinction between freemen and slaves by putting all men in the same fundamental situation. This does not imply absolute uniformity. It allows for differences, even certain differences not found in any other context. The very fact that Christian existence rests not upon man and the world but on grace, and that this grace proceeds from the sovereign decision of the living God, rules out such uniformity. What a diversity of characters, what degrees and shades can be discovered from the saints in their solitary grandeur to the ordinary simple level! But these differences lie within the same fundamental situation. All men are God's creatures, they all stand before Him in their guilt, they are all redeemed and called to His adopted sonship. This basic communion in experience is brought out in the impressive words of Ephesians: "Be ye careful to keep the unity of the Spirit…as you are called in one hope of your calling. One Lord, one faith, one baptism. One God and Father of all, who is above all, and through all, and in us all" (4:5–6). In this unity there is "neither Jew nor Greek, neither bond nor free, neither male nor female, for you are all one in Christ Jesus" (Gal. 3:28). The distinction which antiquity had attached to work disappears. It is no longer shameful for it is part of man's life as such; it is even made an obligation as a means of placing oneself in obedience in God's sight.

At this point, the Northern peoples make their inroad into Western history. The man of the South has, of course, within himself the tensions and contradictions belonging to human nature, but despite that he has a certain special harmony of his own, owing in great part to the balance he achieves between soul and body. The soul expresses itself directly through the body and the body is under the immediate formative influence of the soul. The result is that Southern humanity which realizes a certain degree of natural harmony with itself, with Nature, and with culture. Everything moves more smoothly and has its satisfying form. An instinctive sense of proportion and a moderation, expressed in varying types of culture, make life run easily and appear "natural." This attitude has of course its reverse side. Things tend to become simplified and superficial. The man from the North is differently constructed. His body and spirit do not associate so harmoniously with one another. Frequently they hinder and contradict each other and take up opposite positions to the extent of being mutually unjust. This renders life more difficult even if it is more energetic and earnest. There enters into everything an element of conflict that can verge upon the catastrophic. The cleavage between spirit and Nature, between man and the demands of civilization, is continuously deepened. Northern man lacks the sense of proportion and the moderation of the South. His will stretches out towards the unlimited and the unconditional. And all of this lends a particular seriousness to his work.

The culture of the Middle Ages was ultimately based on the knight and priest, and thus, in spite of a desire for property, its main significance was not in the economic order. Work formed a part of a recognizable structure which prevented its last consequences from being drawn. At the close of the Middle Ages leadership passed to the towns, that is, to the townsman. In contrast to the idealism of knight and priest, he developed a new realism; he replaced a characteristic attitude founded upon metaphysical concepts with one of practical achievement. There emerged the economic outlook of the townsman, determined to acquire wealth, to enrich himself, and to dominate through his riches, to wit, Capitalism. As Max Weber and Werner Sombart have indicated, strong religious forces were at work in this movement. Protestantism made faith so exclusively the one foundation for Christian life that its links with the world were snapped and the world became a free sphere of activity for man's domination. Man wanted to establish some guarantee and pledge of Divine favour, and he frequently discovers this in bourgeois-economic prosperity, with the consequence that efficiency and achievement are made religious values. Work is regarded as the methodical and conscientious effort on which human existence is established, which is directed towards actual mastery of the world and brings with it material prosperity. The entire social order is inspired by this fundamental principle, and work is made the indispensable law for the individual; he must undertake work, even against his will.

This view reaches its culmination at the beginning of the nineteenth century with the final triumph of the natural sciences and the rise of technology. The economic motive is reinforced by the scientific, technical motive, that is to say, the determination to dominate Nature and to give it a new shape. Previously, with all his artistic creativeness, man had left Nature very much as it was, with its clearly defined and not too remote boundaries; he now breaks up the natural structure with his scientific knowledge and technical methods, forces his way to its constituent elements and disposes of them. As will be seen in the following section, he thus gathers an ever-increasing power of control. This will to power objectivizes itself and becomes a will to existence as a whole. From it there spring tasks that increase in magnitude and make more and more difficult demands upon man's strength. The result is our modern man, a *man of work*, who, obsessed by this economic and technical urge for domination, applies his whole strength to secure this world dominion, but at one and the same time he is made the servant of these enterprises and has to labour incessantly in that service.

The consequences of this crisis concerning the nature of work are now made apparent; there is one from the religious aspect. As the new age develops, it becomes more and more estranged from religion. Faith grows feebler in the lives of its leading individuals and classes. Man's refusal to administer the world in subjection to God becomes more decisive, and he claims with growing vehemence to be himself its undisturbed overlord. In the process he loses the transcendence of himself that derives from faith and he loses the ability to see anything except the world and its ambitions. This renders the appeal of work and the necessity for work even more irresistible. He also forgets all those acts and attitudes that may be comprised under the general name of "contemplative": the power not only to rest from strenuous activity but also to live in repose; the capacity for living free from utilitarian aims; and all contact with what is interior, lofty, and eternal.

And now that he has finally been made the captive of work, what is he to do when not working? He can only enjoy himself, and once again, since there is no transcendence to protect him, he does so slavishly and from necessity. Once he has abandoned the pursuit of work and pleasure, his inner emptiness asserts itself. And therefore all higher motives—personal, ethical, and religious—lead necessarily to work. For him, where the believer finds an association with the living God and with the world, there is an empty void, into which the demon forces his way. The man has the feeling that, along that path, he loses all the more tender and lofty things in life, the faculty of composure and peace, freedom and beauty, inwardness and love, but he is determined to follow it because the will to world dominion—the root of his rebellion against God—has grown to dominate him, because he himself has collapsed in degradation and ruin.

This rhythm of degradation found its appropriate expression in the obsessive character attributed to work during the "twelve years" of Nazi domination. It was accepted as an unconditional value, with self-evident validity. Its purpose was no longer called in question; it was work for work's sake. This was an instance of that formalism that regularly sets in where there is no real content or significance left. With this approach to work, man is in exactly the same position as a person who lacks all material moral values and restricts himself to "preserving the proper external attitude" under all circumstances. It is a mark of bankruptcy.

One consequence of this idolization of work is to convert men into very pliant material for that power which has repudiated God and usurped His rights, the absolute State. And if in addition this State takes upon itself to provide for man the opposite polarity to work, namely, pleasure—again taken for granted and without question—and to strike a balance, objective and subjective, between these two, then the poor, wretched man is finally engulfed to the last detail. This absorption is all the more horrible when the "State" itself is sheer emptiness, when it has lost the marks of sovereignty and right and sunk to the indignity of a pure instrument of power in the hands of thoroughly irresponsible groups and classes, as happened in Germany during the twelve years and is still happening elsewhere.

What escape is there? Only faith.

Man must give honour to God; and, by so doing, he regains that transcendence over himself and his work. Associated with God, he is able to find interior repose and to rediscover that rhythm of life that moves beyond utility to the eternal. Then does work lose its demonic importance. And from the same source man learns to detach himself and make renunciation; the spell of pleasure is broken; freedom begins to dawn once more.

Destiny

THE PROBLEM

We are concerned in this study with three patterns of reality and significance which form the basic texture of existence: freedom, grace, and destiny. Experience brings us into continual contact with what is necessary and immutable but also with what is original and spontaneous. It is always coming into contact with a transparent and calculable element but also with a further element beyond our powers of compulsion and in itself a gift. To trace either of these two phenomena is to wander through the three dimensions—the height, breadth, and depth—of existence. Our question must now be directed towards the third of these significant patterns, namely, destiny. It was not easy to speak of the first two. The mind could penetrate a certain distance into their content but then it lost itself in a hopeless impasse. It will be even more difficult to inquire into destiny.

Whatever answer we can give will be inadequate and, if measured by a strict, conceptual standard, rather vague, yet it may be useful. To work it out, we must proceed along the lines adopted in the two preceding sections. We must first ask how this phenomenon of destiny is presented in immediate experience; then, what God's revelation has to tell us about it, concluding with a number of suggestions on the significance of revelation for our direct experience of destiny.

ROMANO GUARDINI

THE ELEMENTS OF OUR EXPERIENCE OF DESTINY

Necessity

As soon as I pronounce the word "destiny" I have the feeling that what it denotes affects me intimately but that it comes from a remote distance. It belongs to my intimate being and yet is strange to me. I know it because I partake of it at my deepest level but it disappears if I try to lay hold of it. It is aimed directly at me but its roots are in a distant soil. Basically, it is the whole of existence. It is at once the core of my personal being, where I stand alone and cannot be represented by another or displaced, and what links me with Being as a whole.

It is difficult, perhaps impossible, for the mind to deal with this question. In any case, we can make no progress without simplification and all we can hope for are some general lines to help us focus the picture to some extent. Then inevitably the mind will lose the focus and have to rest content with a strange, mysterious outline.

If after some shattering experience with far-reaching consequences, or when we have been forced to look back over an important era in our lives, we examine what we understand by "destiny," we observe that its principal note is one of necessity. Destiny, in our experience, is what cannot be changed, what cannot be avoided, what forces itself upon us.

By necessity we understand what we perceive and know must exist; perhaps we also see why it could not exist in any other way. It is built up at different levels. To begin with, clearly and definitely, we have the necessity of the laws of Nature which find their expression in mathematical formulae. A law of Nature is never repealed, providing, that is, that we are dealing with a genuine law of Nature and remain within its proper field of application. Where such a law appears to be cancelled, this means that a higher factor has entered into effect and set it in a new context, as occurs with chemicophysical laws with the advent of life or to biological laws with the entry of spirit. In the new context the law is once again valid, only the manner of its validity is new and more complex.[1] The same is true of the laws of thought. Where you have a genuine logical connection, the evidence shows that, given these presuppositions, it cannot be other than it is. Were the presuppositions to be altered, the logical relations would be different, as in mathematics, once a system of axioms is adopted different from that of our world of direct experience. In this case, however, the former axioms would not be "abrogated" but referred back with the newer axioms to basic principles which they have in common. This is equally true of the laws of psychology, biology, and sociology, and such as can be established by a study of man's historical experience, provided that we are dealing with real "laws" and not merely general directives and that our mind has grasped their true meaning, not merely approximated to them.

This necessity supports and orders our existence. But awareness of it is a relatively later development in the history of mind. It does not appear in the mythological picture of the world, for example, for this represents the whole of reality as an association and conflict between natural, numinous forces not subject to any calculable rules. True, it did include "necessities" which, quite apart from their rightness or wrongness, we are no longer in a position to notice: the associations expressed

---

1. Even a miracle is no exception. The belief that a miracle cannot happen because it would abrogate the laws of Nature is based on a misunderstanding. When a miracle actually occurs, the laws of Nature are not "abrogated"; they are taken in hand by the sovereign will of the Lord of the world and made to achieve an effect that their ordinary operation in the world could not demand. This emphasis on God's sovereign will should remind us that the laws of Nature are not rules of behaviour but are the truth. Truth cannot be abrogated, it can only be placed in a new context. It is precisely because natural truth is orientated directly towards the realization of God's kingdom through God's special initiative that we can have a genuine miracle, as distinct from magic and wonders.

in myths with their images and processes, and their symbolic representation in cults. These contained the meaning, arranged the sequence, and guaranteed the order of existence. The man who understood them could control existence, especially by means of magical practices which men were convinced exercised a direct influence upon the interplay of these forces. This mythological picture of the world vanished as man came to know the orderly arrangement of natural events. Its disappearance involved the loss of a certain grandeur but there disappeared at the same time that disturbing anxiety in which human life had been steeped—a fact easily forgotten by admirers of this mythology. The insight into the orderly pattern of Nature sobered man but gave him also a new freedom and dignity.

Necessity can be felt as constraint and compulsion against which individual life rebels, as, for instance, when disastrous consequences follow on the fulfilment of some action. But it may also be recognized as a support and protection. We need only imagine what would happen if we could not rely on the laws of Nature. There are certain pathological conditions which give us a fair idea of what that situation might be.[2] Our whole life is based upon the fact that there are no exceptions to the orderly pattern of being, thought, and action. On this we rely absolutely. But as far as freedom is concerned, it stands in a special relation to law. Where it does not understand it or rebels against it, law is felt as constrictive. But where the free will aims not at arbitrary objectives but

2. We have in the first place those strange experiences in which habitual activities, like walking or the sequence of act and effect or of breathing and heartbeats, lose their normal unconscious status and become objects of consciousness and seem to be threatened. Philosophically, this experience gives a deeper insight into reality; from the medical or pedagogical standpoint it puts the doctor or teacher into contact with the basic structure of life. But when it grows intense, it impairs the power of action or even life itself. Many an artistic creation like the writing of Dostoyevsky or the painting of Van Gogh belongs to this border country between the land where life is possible and the further land where it is no longer so.

at what is just and right, grasping the meaning of what is lawful—even though it may have to trust another's judgment—freedom will enter into correspondence with law and find itself corroborated by it.

We have the natural conviction that the various aspects of necessity are linked with one another. Individual patterns of law fit into more comprehensive patterns, and these in their turn into still wider and more embracing patterns. Individual laws may mutually dissolve one another or they may retain a fundamental characteristic that will show itself differently in different realms of reality. Experience shows that no law is in real contradiction with any other, however foreign it may seem, provided that in each case we are dealing with genuine laws and that the different standpoints and spheres of application are properly considered. This consideration, with others, compels the assumption that all these laws form an ultimate unity which no doubt surpasses our comprehension—an order that does not disturb the manifold variety of Being, preserving the distinction between living and inanimate, between freedom and necessity, but provides the preconditions of its stability and links it with the "world" as a whole.

The Fact

A second element in destiny is *fact*, that is, everything which cannot be seen to exist necessarily but does exist *de facto*; in other words, fact is everything that proceeds from freedom. It is done because the agent wills to do it. It might not have been willed. But, once willed and put into effect, it is there irrevocably.

Facts emerge continually from my individual life. The words I utter, the gestures I make, the change of circumstances that I bring about—these are facts. So too are the operations caused by my thoughts, words, and acts within myself: their influence on my attitude, my habits, my character, and finally their continued presence in my memory.

Psychology shows that there is an unconscious as well as a conscious memory and that it apparently never forgets the content of any experience or act, with the result that every event remains a "factum" in my life. My active, creative initiative objectivizes itself continuously in such "facts." The older I am, the more facts—whether they be decisions, statements, actions, forms—are grouped within my sphere of life, the more tightly knit is their association, and therefore it is all the more difficult to keep them flexible or to break through them. They peg down my initiative, and all the more so since the process of assembling them goes on unnoticed.

The same is true of history. Historical facts accumulate and collect together in patterns that have a remarkable stability. In them are objectivized the joint initiative of the various groups in human life, families, clans, tribes, peoples, and associations of peoples. We must understand the important and decisive part played in history by genuine fact. There is a modern tendency, a blend of Idealistic theory and Positivist concentration on matter, that is always finding necessary processes. The standpoint is both false and dangerous: false, because at every step freedom is operating; dangerous, in that it discourages initiative and removes a sense of responsibility. History occurs as it does, not because it has to but because it is the result of will, on a grand scale at critical moments but always to a certain though smaller extent. The resulting pattern of facts will be larger and more closely interwoven, the longer that history continues, and it becomes increasingly difficult to penetrate them and keep them in movement. Finally, existence itself, the world and myself in the world—all this, as we have insisted previously, is fact. The world did not have to be what it is; now that it is so, it is irrevocably so. It did not even have to exist at all; but now that it does exist, it is irretrievably there. Once it is as it is, it includes necessity, the complex of laws that order it, but nothing can convince me that the world with all these necessities must itself necessarily exist. It exists because it has been fashioned by the creator's act.[3] This original *act-fact* condition of things is continually renewed within the world by human freedom. If the world as a whole were not constituted as an *act-fact* through freedom, there would be no possibility of freedom within it. The modern concept of Nature which denies its *act-factual* character would be compelled logically to repudiate freedom. If the world as a whole must necessarily exist, then everything in it exists with the same necessity.

This factual element poses a difficult problem for human initiative. It is freedom's task to master reality. It finds this relatively easy in the case of necessity, when it is properly guided and understands, directly or indirectly, the meaning of the natural laws. In the last resort, it can never desire that the necessities were not there, for in that case everything would subside into chaos, and chaos implies the absence of meaning and therefore enslavement. But such a connection is not present in dealing with facts. I cannot see that a fact must exist but only that it does exist. It is just there. If it helps me, I regard it as favourable and respond thankfully; if it hurts me, it seems an evil and awakens in me a feeling of annoyance and self-defence. A fact has to be mastered differently from necessity. A man must continually appropriate what exists and fit it into his life pattern. And, to begin with, he must do this with his own self. He must accept the fact that this is his disposition, these are his capacities and failings, these his possibilities and limits. He is faced with the earnest challenge to be what he is, to reach an agreement with himself, and to remain patient with himself, when all the time imagination outsoars reality. We see here at once the helpful and the insidious activity of imagination, dream and intoxication, free play and concealment; for

3. In the German text there is a play on the words *Tat* (*act*) and *Sache* (reality, thing), which results in the combined word: *Tat-Sache* (the *fact* that is the result of an *act*).

a short spell they create the illusion that we can slough off the fetters of our factual selves and become other persons, to realize in the end more forcibly how impossible this is. One of the most pressing tasks of our moral life is to take charge of ourselves, with great energy at certain critical moments and in a general manner throughout normal existence. This is not resignation but the truth of existence and it is the precondition of all honest effort. In the same way, a man must shoulder responsibility for the consequences of his action, the facts which he has brought into being and accumulated. And this again is not an attitude of fatalism towards the past but a means of making ourselves upright in our lives and providing a stepping stone for the future.

What is true of the individual is true again of history. Historical activity produces an ever-growing mountain of facts which are then every bit as real as natural data and they condition future action. At each moment the historical present has to take over and master the inheritance of the past. It must resolve its conflicts, direct its stored energies, bring to maturity forms that have been active within it, encouraging those that have been progressive and rejecting others in favour of fresher and more vital facts. This challenge can often be arduous, especially when past dishonesty and insolence have bequeathed a heritage of evil imprisonment for their heirs. It is no easy choice to determine whether to make a clean break or to blunt one's conscience, as though nothing had occurred, make a detour or take some short cut, with the result that the same disastrous consequences are continued.

Facts constitute also a system of relations. In the individual this is the design and burden of life; in a group existence, the complex of all that a people or group of peoples or humanity as a whole does, creates, experiences and what, in short, becomes "history." And since all that exists finds its ultimate definition in man, this means "the world" in the full sense.

This system of relations cannot be fathomed. But its lack of transparency differs from the complex laws we have been discussing. It is not only too extensive or too profound or too complicated, but here the mind comes up against the reality that the *fact*, that is, what does not necessarily exist yet actually exists, cannot be deduced, and the problem is made more acute by the folly and evil in man's will. Hence the alarming questions: Why is life as it is? Why have men behaved as they have actually behaved? Why is there life at all, and activity?[4] These questions can never be answered purely from the facts but only from God, who established the world as "act-fact." And although insight into the patterned relation of necessity could provide us with that final insight, perspective, and survey that science and philosophy are always seeking, history, if it is to be rightly understood, requires a *judgment*.[5]

Chance

Facts assume a special character when they appear in the form of chance. From what has already been said it is evident that there is no absolute chance. That would presuppose something grounded neither in the patterned necessity of things nor in responsible freedom. There exists, however, this feeling of chance which is also a genuine experience of a "gift." It affects a man's sphere of life and is felt when something occurs in that sphere that does not fit in with the general pattern: for example, a strange encounter from some far-away source or, in general, some harmony of exterior circumstance and personal plan without any causes that can be discovered.

4. This mood is expressed with exceptional sensitiveness in the poetry of Giacomo Leopardi. I recall for instance his melancholy *Canto notturno di un pastore* (Shepherd's Song During the Night) and the powerful elegy, *La Ginestra* (The Broom). (Cf. *Opere*, ed. R. Bachelli and G. Scarpa [Milan, 1935], vol. 1, 63 and 95.)

5. For a more detailed treatment, see pp. 188ff.

This note of chance may be heightened. It may become absurd, when an insignificant cause, perhaps a slight mistake, brings disastrous results; it may be unjust, as when an action leads to unethical consequences, for instance, when evil follows from an act performed with the best intentions; it may become objectively evil and malicious, for example, where a petty occurrence destroys great work or misfortune keeps intervening to paralyse a noble disposition.

The problem of chance provides the greatest obstacle for an understanding of existence for it confuses the meaning of life. To some extent, the experience may be a positive one; it reminds us that life is unpredictable, and this compels man to remain continually on the watch and to meet every move of life with an even more rapid defensive reaction. There have existed periods when this feeling was exceptionally vivid: the Renaissance, for instance, with its concept of Fortuna, mixing and confounding human affairs in wholly unreasonable moods, destroying the weaklings and forcing the strong to use every ounce of their vitality. The same age was keenly interested in stranger and more abnormal aspects of life, and had a love of adventure and a keen zest for the discovery of wonderful things. But, this apart, chance is felt to be a lack of order; a muddled, malicious, and wicked note appears in it. If we inquire how this came to be, we become conscious of an original guilt which, reinforced continually by new guilt, has confused the significant relations of human life, and we are compelled to postulate forces hostile to it, which either exercise direct power over it or use man's guilt as a breach through which to penetrate into its general structure.

Destiny in Man Himself

Destiny has its basis in the entire length and breadth of the world and history. This we recognize easily if we trace back the lines of development of some event that has affected us. I applied for some post—to take an instance—and did not get it. For this there are grounds in myself, and these have their precedent grounds in my action, milieu, education, descent, and so forth. There are grounds also in the persons who made the decision, which in turn have preceding grounds both in the individual and more generally. The connections soon multiply and spread till they become lost in space and time. When I seek the original cause as that which emerges where destiny meets existence, then I am brought back to immediate experience. Destiny fulfils itself as it proceeds from the totality beyond my ken through the various layers of my immediate world and draws near to myself. The point of occurrence is in myself, my individual existence, more precisely, in my person.

In the final sense, destiny is the impact of reality upon myself. This statement calls to mind an essential element which we have hitherto ignored. We have been considering destiny only from its objective aspect as what confronts man. But in fact it proceeds also from man himself. After all, he is part of reality, the most immediate and, for himself, the most effective part.

Necessity also is found in man, in all the various patterns which determine his physical, psychological, and spiritual being. These form the basis of his individual existence, determine his place in the grand whole, his special character, his possibilities and his limits. They therefore create a destiny for him in the strict sense. We have noted how actions continually proceed from man's freedom and how their consequences are preserved in his sphere of life as facts and they in their turn fashion a destiny. What is not so clear is the presence of chance in man. This has been defined as what does not consciously and intelligently fit into the conceptual framework of a man's life. But what, we may ask, is the real content of this life? First of all, what I myself know, perceive, and achieve through action, in other words, my conscious existence. But not everything occurring in me belongs to this system. There are elements which give the impression of forcing their way into it from elsewhere and not really fitting into it. This is true enough, only this "elsewhere" is inside my own being. Psychology informs me that my existence does not coincide with what I can directly know in self-awareness or when I search my memory or analyse the motives of my action but that, on the contrary, regions exist within myself that are beyond the reach of knowledge of this kind and can be revealed only in a round-about manner and through special techniques, namely, the realms of the subconscious and unconscious. These have wide ramifications, and they are not only present, they also operate. They form the deeper level of my life as a whole, and this supports, nourishes, controls, and directs its upper layers; it also disturbs, thwarts, and misleads them. It is the source of those impulses, hindrances, disturbances, premonitions, and reliefs that irrupt into my conscious life without showing any logical connection with it, for instance, a premonition, something that saves the situation, a sudden return of self-confidence. At times they break in as strangely and suddenly as an event from outside, and this, as we understand it, means by chance. There are moments when this note is intensified to the point of disorderliness, mischief, and malicious destruction, for example, in various forms of failure that can affect a person's life most acutely. It can be heightened to such a degree that the man has the sensation of being dominated, tormented, and crushed by powers or beings foreign to himself, as in the different forms of psychological illness ranging from simple compulsion to a feeling of being possessed.

The significance of the self in creating what we know as destiny is an even more profound one. In terms of involuntary feeling, it is what confronts me as though from outside. If I am assured that what confronts me arises from hidden regions in my own life, this means in the first place that I regard my psychophysical existence as a portion of reality, namely, interior reality, and that my personal initiative comes into contact with the material of existence on that side also. But there is even more that calls for notice. I am actively engaged in creating my destiny in so far as I select and direct the events which come my way. It might seem unnecessary to stress this as we dealt with it when considering the results of freedom. Here we are treating that problem from a different point of view.

A notion drawn from biology and sociology may be of service. An individual does not live simply in the external world as a whole; out of it he fashions a narrower sphere, his own particular world, or *Umwelt*.[6] This happens through the organization of his senses which lets him perceive one particular object and not another, so that the former is part of his immediate world whereas the latter, though actually present, is not part of his world. There is a similar phenomenon in his physiological state, his needs and impulses, the structure and range of his organs, his temperament, character, and special capacity. In all these respects the individual fashions his own world out of the world-stuff as a whole—nourishment and self-preservation, dress and ornament, house and work, family, circles of friends, and social level. A further process may be discovered in human behaviour. What happens to a man does not, in the main, happen by chance; it stands in essential relation to him. Even what comes upon him suddenly from the general pattern of events is determined by the fact that *he* is the person affected. From the stuff of reality he appropriates a realm of events that belong to and are related to himself. It is true that these are determined by the objective realities of Nature, history, and society, that is, "from outside," but at the same

6. Translator's Note: The term *Umwelt* indicates the particular setting or milieu in which a being is situated; it is that portion of external reality necessary and proper to itself and, to use the terminology of Heidegger, this *Umwelt* is essentially subordinate to man; it is his world of tools and instruments that serve his purposes and it exists only in that instrumental capacity. To be distinguished from this *Umwelt* of objects is man's *Mitwelt*, in which he co-exists with other human beings.

time they are constituted "from within" through himself. His particular personality is based upon family environment and individual disposition, education and accepted ideals. He has therefore his own attitude to external events and he influences them in his own way. This individual sphere of action colours his efforts to protect himself against disturbing elements and to welcome those that are favourable, to bring order and pattern into his life, in short, whatever belongs to the control and the art of living. Beneath conscious activity there is another and unconscious activity which can be detected only through indirect analysis and yet it exercises an influence on personal behaviour: among instances are the fixed attitudes which determine the direction of sympathy and antipathy; basic tendencies directing concrete action; unresolved tensions that have penetrated into our basic structure and work themselves out in relation with other human beings; behaviour patterns springing from previous experience and unconsciously followed. It becomes evident that much of what at first seems to derive wholly from outside is in effect willed by the unconscious self and directed at times with remarkable assurance.

These attitudes and activities are all closely related. They are determined by an inner form, an *entelechy*, based in part upon the individual personality and in part created by education and decisive experience. This is the form from which proceed the individual's self-expression and self-development. Continuously and effectively it influences interior and exterior attitudes and fashions both the individual and his *Umwelt.* The process is not purely natural as with a plant or animal. Man has a spiritual element so that this form is not only the principle from which he operates but also a task that has to be fulfilled. Even this does not quite bring out the distinction because it is part of an organism to realize itself during the course of its growth. In man, on the other hand, this self-realization belongs to freedom. His essential form is therefore the basis of his reality and his purpose. It must be fulfilled through conquest, superficial elements must be sacrificed to deeper factors, crises have to be sustained and tensions resolved. Freedom can face these demands or run away from them; it can correspond with this essential form of life or do violence to it. And so the order of which we have been speaking receives a note of its own: it becomes a living conscience which lays down the right rule of behaviour, attaches a moral value to it and recognizes guilt when it is unfaithful to it, and attempts to punish or compensate for it. This complex situation touches freedom at its core where both constructive and conserving and also disturbing and destructive tendencies are operative. It is a mysterious condition of things, only to be finally explained in terms of revelation, especially through the doctrine of original sin and its consequences. These have disrupted the pattern of life, and this has resulted in insecurity, contradictions, and diseased phenomena of various kinds. Ethically, it has resulted in the confusion of a false as well as a sound conscience, and this falsity does not derive exclusively from mistaken judgment; it may spring from an interior corruption.

As has been noted, the form of life exercises a profound influence upon what happens to the individual man. It makes him highly sensitive to certain external influences, less sensitive or perhaps quite insensitive to others. It puts him in a position in which he can consciously react to definite men, relations, and situations and it facilitates these relations and reactions while he remains unaffected by other situations or rejects them as hostile. The impact of other men and of Nature upon a particular person is largely conditioned or at least made possible by his own behaviour; consequently, this inner form of life is responsible for his way of behaviour. To this we have finally to add all that the psychology of the unconscious tells us about luck and failure, assurance and mischance, about the concrescence of chance happenings and the rise

of many nervous and even organic diseases.[7] All these tendencies func-
146 tion so regularly and surely that the form which regulates them may be described as interior destiny.

Yet we must repeat that it does not function with any purely natural necessity. It certainly creates my sphere of possible action and the way in which my activity is realized, in both a good and a bad sense. This is proved by every act of self-conquest and in every act in which I am false to my true self. Yet the evidence for it remains somewhat incalculable. I experience it as a force that can give assurance and help or that can endanger and destroy, and not merely as something that presses upon me from within; it descends upon me from outside. The figure at the centre of this experience is myself; it is the entelechy of my concrete existence. Yet it has been realized only partially in my past life; it remains in part as a future possibility, and in this respect also it influences my present reality. It appears as something other than myself that comes to meet me, as a foreign power moving towards me, and at times as an overpowering force or doom. It is the entelechy of my individual being but it is also, to some extent, that of the various groups to which I belong: family, friends, working associates, social class, people, State, and Church. It is at once within me and yet outside me, and in this second capacity it

7. The psychology of accidents and of organic diseases is most illuminating. An accident, to begin with, seems to be something fully objective and withdrawn from the person's will. But analysis reveals that it is not only affected by the characteristic attitude of the person but also that is often carefully directed or even produced by the unconscious self and from motives which form part of his life pattern. The study of nervous and organic diseases affords further evidence. These too may be brought about by the unconscious self—for instance, in an attempt to escape infection—and their development can be controlled by it. In its research into the formation of destiny psychology must take note that voluntary movements in the organism, such as the use of limbs and sense organs, are regulated by the conscious psyche whereas involuntary movements like breathing, the action of the heart, and metabolic processes are to a large extent regulated by the unconscious psyche. Destiny accordingly consists, in large measure, in the right or wrong functioning of these movements, that is, in healthy or diseased conditions.

confronts me as a factor that is foreign but that affects me and gains a hold over me that may be intensified to the point of overthrow or doom.

THE RELIGIOUS AND THE PERSONAL ELEMENTS IN THE EXPERIENCE OF DESTINY

The Religions Character of Destiny

The various elements we have been analysing form the general pattern that we term destiny. Or, more precisely, destiny presents itself in experience as an original unity from which it is possible to isolate these different elements. To repeat, they include, in the first place, necessity—the orderly disposition of being and process, the necessity of whose pattern I can perceive. This permeates all reality down to its slightest details. It sustains existence and gives it security but it confines it within a framework from which it cannot escape. Next there is *fact*—that which exists but in whose existence I can detect no necessity—the factuality of existence, as inevitable as its necessity, yet impermeable to thought. It consists of the world's reality as such which cannot be deduced from any principles and of everything that is produced by freedom, that is, historical reality in the strict sense. This is what for me is particularly "given," produced, and its final inevitability is the most difficult problem in destiny. These two elements do not exist side by side; necessities are active in the factuality of existence as facts in their turn are grounded in the orderly pattern. When I reflect upon the facts from my particular standpoint, their factual character is sometimes made more precise. They are seen not merely as what is impenetrable and must therefore be accepted but also as having a quite irrational relation to a cause and significance, namely, chance, arbitrariness, and malice. Destiny therefore acquires the notes of resistance to calculation, understanding and goodness. It becomes blind and evil. And

this additional note runs parallel with the others but it also permeates the
148 whole and often seems to be its most fundamental characteristic.[8]

Destiny comes to me from outside, yet it is already present within myself. Not, however, as if I were completely formed before destiny approached me from the outside, from Nature and history. I am myself my own destiny. My living self is continually fulfilling its laws, bringing facts into existence, and meeting with chance events. I go on determining what seem objective presentations; I select, appropriate, and direct certain acts of the manifold variety of behaviour. Destiny is the strangeness of the world that moves towards me, the onrush as of a hostile force; but it is at the same time akin to me and my very own. It denotes both a power transcending my existence and the form in which I realize myself.

This does not give us, however, the whole problem of destiny but merely its direct material and structure. Behind it lies a further factor which reveals and conceals itself in this material. This emerges most clearly from those questions containing the words ""Why" and "I" that are quite insoluble: "Why does this happen precisely to me?" "Why may I, and why must I, be the person I am?" "Why do I exist at all?"[9] These suggest an element of mystery in destiny. I am not here referring to the

---

8. Cf. Leopardi in the short poem *A se stesso* (To Himself):
   Al gener nostro il fato
   Non donò che il morire. Ormai disprezza
   Te, la natura, il brutto
   Poter, che, nascoso, a comun danno impera,
   E l'infinita vanità dei tutto. (*Opere*, 1.77.)
   ("To human kind fate has decreed nothing but death.
   Scorn now thyself, and Nature, and that brutal power
   That, hidden, governs to the universal hurt,
   And the infinite vanity of all things.")
9. These are the questions that provide the deepest element in melancholy. And melancholy brings with it the sense that existence cannot be understood. Again, I recall Leopardi's elegy, *Canto notturno,* in which this mood of melancholy assumes a positive shape and figure. (*Opere*, 1.77.)

unsolved and perhaps insoluble problem but to mystery as a quality of being, the element of the numinous. It is the same factor that we met in inquiring into the origin of graciousness.[10] Were it possible to show exactly how experience of this graciousness could be reduced to definite psychological or personal causes, then the inquirer might feel that the question had been solved. But he would soon realize that either the question had been misunderstood or that an essential element had been omitted.[11] He would conclude that the ground of the gracious occurrence must have a special note and so reach the note of the religious, which does not postulate any other note behind it but just has to be accepted as an original datum. Similarly, we do not answer the question whence proceeds the orderly pattern of existence by enumerating all the natural factors. We must always feel painfully aware that destiny comes from a sphere impossible to approach, the sphere in which religious forces operate. The mystery we sense in destiny is qualitatively distinct. It lies within and also behind and above every actual empirical cause. It operates and expresses itself in the necessities, facts, and chance incidents already mentioned and these receive their special character from it.

Finally, what I experience in destiny is something numinous. It is charged with mysterious energy and it wields power over me. It "wills" something from me or against me or above me. The necessities of law express a power which I cannot influence. In facts a "will" is revealed which makes them what they are, without letting me see the reason why, and it sustains them, however strongly my own will may run up against them. And chance that can touch the extreme of meaninglessness shows

10. Cf. pp. 95ff.

11. This brings out the blindness of Positivism, which imagines that it can treat religious questions as a pure puzzle to be explained rationally. It confuses the qualitatively mysterious with problems not yet solved. Apart from this, it has a mania for unmasking and destroying which springs from its basic approach to existence.

me that the operation of this power is not always intelligible in the sense
150 normally accepted by my mind and heart. There are in addition the movements of destiny from that strange realm I cannot penetrate. These may have a good meaning and frequently I think I can grasp it.[12] But often this meaning appears impure, hostile, and evil. There are times when I feel that the point of destiny is that it bears no relation at all to anything that I regard as normative, as though it has no conceivable meaning and just occurs without rhyme or reason.

This note of strangeness represents the mysterious element in things which we call the numinous. Men have always interpreted destiny in this way, as long as their religion has retained its vigour, and even in materialistic and positivist periods it finds its echo in superstition. The history of religions tells us of gods that distribute happiness and unhappiness, of Norns and Fates that spin and then snap the threads of human life. In the last resort, the gods have to act as the power of destiny ordains, and this power is frightening and incalculable, and from it there is no appeal to any higher source.

Something similar is found in man's inner experience. The orderly pattern, the elements of both fact and chance in him, point to something permanent behind them, a mysterious centre, that influences his behaviour and constructs a destiny.[13] A man does not merely sustain and

---

12. In moments when the world pattern and one's own will mutually illuminate one another and "everything" becomes lucid. Such moments often have a quality of euphoria so that the two phenomena of destiny and graciousness intermingle. But these lucid moods cannot be objectivized; they remain incapable of expression. They are also attached to this or the other moment and vanish when it passes. Afterwards I remain aware that I did understand something of importance but not what it was.

13. This receives strong confirmation from Jung's theory of significant centres in the unconscious self which give rise to myths; cf. K. Kerényi and C. G. Jung, *Essays on a Science of Mythology*. It may be objected, however, that the theory does not confine itself to psychological elements, where it would be justified, but drags in every aspect of life.

adapt a destiny coming from outside but he creates this destiny himself, as expressed in the ideas of personal salvation or happiness or, on the contrary, in those of loss and wretchedness, and these notions have a far wider range than the mere fact that the individual is favoured or disadvantaged by destiny. It is a question of the individual's own strength, ultimately a numinous quality, which confronts objective destiny and fulfils it.[14]

Awareness of destiny is based upon our experience of an ultimate order and wisdom and also on the opposite concept of destiny as arbitrary, envious, blind, and meaningless. This twofold approach is constantly to be observed in myths and legends and also in dreams, in the movements of a sick psyche, and generally in the involuntary expressions of life. Man feels himself threatened by it. He must not challenge destiny but hide from it what is best in himself, stave it off and outmanoeuvre it. The alternative is to discover a centre in his own being that will combat destiny and, even should he suffer defeat and destruction, would feel that combat well justified.

At its most profound level, this sense of destiny seems to contain an even darker element, the sense of an evil rejection of truth and goodness, an element that is Satanic. It finds an outlet in various kinds of demonism, as they continually recur in religions and in the forces of destruction and cruelty, frightfulness and terror. Our modern aesthetics claim that this should be accepted as a constitutive factor in being. In point of fact, it can never be accepted because what it does elicit is the exact contrary: it is cold, evil, heartless, and empty—but as an "other"

14. Cf. G. van der Leeuw on both the subjective and objective life of the soul, *Phänomenologie der Religion* (1933), pp. 276ff.; also W. Groenbech, *Kultur und Religion der Germanen* (1937–1939), I, pp. 105ff. At a higher and more skilful level we find Hellenistic *Heimarmene* harmonized with *Nous* and its objective validity and with *Sophrosyne* within the morally active man.

also belonging to the religious sphere, though in the bad sense, and it can claim no reverence except from the warped and the perverted.

This element does not make its significance evident. It springs from the confusion in existence, it mingles with the good and conceals itself behind what does have meaning and significance. Its proper character was first made known by revelation and finally through Christ.

The Subject of This Experience of Destiny

As in the case of freedom, so in this question of destiny we must inquire who experiences and fulfils it. Certainly, not everything. A star can no more have destiny than a river or a stone. To attribute it to such things would be a mere personification, due to a primitive belief in a universal soul giving life and will to all objects. Destiny requires initiative, but again, not in the manner in which all living beings, capable of suffering and death, possess it. If a young tree, fair and full of promise, is destroyed or a noble animal is killed we may perhaps discover a kind of destiny in this but that is to read our own experience into it. By initiative we mean in the first place freedom, as analysed in the first section of this book, and this presupposes a living spirit.

Only a spiritual being endowed with freedom can sense how inevitable are necessary things for it alone can feel their sustenance or opposition. With its creative imagination it transcends the limits of necessity and yet it is compelled to adapt itself to them. Only a free being that craves for an insight into the significance of things can feel and therefore react against the stern reality of facts. Yet, seen from another point of view, only a free being is capable of discovering the meaning of destiny in the friendly approach of existence and its kindly design.

All this is epitomized in the notion of person. Personality is that manner of existing-within-oneself (*In-sich-selbst-stehen*) in which the self-conscious and free spirit belongs to itself. Only a person can have destiny.

Destiny denotes correspondence and proportion. It gives man his place in existence, his material and degree of life, possibilities and limits for fulfilment and failure. But it signifies also a task for his individual action and creation. Man is entrusted with the task of fashioning his own world, the world that develops as he comes to know, adopt attitudes towards, and deal with objective data, a world of reality as observed, assessed, experienced, and fashioned. This world emerges from each man's life; it corresponds to the number of men and to their rich variety. Destiny lays down its possibilities and its limits. In destiny the world confronts man as that which is *given* in order that from it he may bring forth the world which it is his task and responsibility to create.

Man's special privilege is that he has the power to answer this appeal. He can do so only because he is a person. For only as a person can he make this response and fulfil it or maybe refuse to listen to it and waste his opportunity. In this latter instance, so far as in him lay, he has gambled away the "world."

THE CONQUEST OF DESTINY

The Support of Destiny, Struggle with Destiny, and the Influence of Its Source

The attempts to deal with destiny are as manifold as the ways in which it is experienced. To analyse them would be to bring the whole problem up again and consequently we must content ourselves with a few suggestions.

To deal first with the Positivists. A man can know that he is supported by destiny. He has this feeling: "I can do this. What I decide on, succeeds. Things accommodate themselves to me. I'm never unfortunate." Such judgments transcend the empirical content of the action or process and in it a more profound note is detected, a correspondence between the individual will and the action of destiny. The man feels the prevailing forces to be friendly and helpful, he believes that his own being springs from them and that he can act with assurance. The gracious element manifests itself within this framework of destiny and it is expressed in the figure of Fortune, in reverence for the stars and his personal lucky star, in the protective influence of powerful ancestors, in the guardian spirit of individual and group and so forth. Psychologically, this experience reveals a profound self-unity, a harmony of conscious and unconscious life, and therefore a correspondence of the conscious will with the natural tendencies of things, the movement of the situation, and the historical moment, all of which may be more profoundly seized by the unconscious will.

Good fortune and success are signs of proportion or balance. They involve the mutual interpenetration of visible and invisible factors, a resolute action which is sensitive to warnings of danger, an independence of choice which yet harmonizes with its object; they demand a blend of energy and caution, of initiative and modesty. No sooner does a man lose this nicely poised proportion than his courage and sense of security disappear or he becomes self-centred and self-confident. The delicate mutual balance exists no longer. His judgment is overclouded. His relation to men and things is lost. Mistake after mistake is committed with consequences which further worsen the situation. Good fortune vanishes, to be succeeded not by an average, ordinary state of affairs but by ill fortune, in which everything works unfavourably.

Good fortune brings life to its full blossom. A happy freedom is established and man's powers of action and creation radiate an air of confidence. Every human life needs some touch of this if it is to thrive properly. Types like the man dogged by misfortune—the man who has no luck or, at a deeper level, the unfortunate and unhappy man—show us what life can be like if it lacks this element altogether, whether the man was born to be unfortunate or his chances of good fortune were lost through his unconscious self or he is so completely out of touch with the age in which he lives that he can find no home in it.

Man may resist destiny, first and foremost with regard to empirical circumstances. The structure of any particular situation and the general framework of life are never hard and fast. As has been observed, they consist not of necessities to which a man must conform himself but of facts to which his freedom may be applied, of forces he can direct, conditions he can fashion, of fluid material he can hold together and obstacles he can overcome. Indeed, this struggle occupies a considerable portion of daily existence. "Life" implies that man has the power to penetrate the stuff of reality—objects, persons, and circumstances—and draw them into his own concrete self. But this stuff of reality has its own form with its own significance and position and it asserts itself. It resists formation by a human will, seals itself off defensively, withdraws and flees. This resistance to will is "destiny" and every attempt to build up the individual involves struggle. In this struggle man's forces are developed and his character is firmly established. History is rich with striking instances of this overcoming of destiny. But it demands an intensity of effort and self-denial at times of the most frightening kind; and beyond a certain point such mastery is quite impossible.

Even the numinous forces that make themselves felt beyond the empirical plane can, it would appear, be held off to a certain extent, directed into other channels, and made to yield to pressure. This has been implied already since the numinous factor in destiny does not operate directly and under its own power but in the empirical data of the situation. Courage, wisdom, and patience can handle these in such a way as to alter its fundamental direction. This theme is exemplified in the heroes and liberators of the ancient epics. The fight with the dragon and unholy forces is in reality the fight with the mythical enemy of life behind the data of experience. Every "natural" manifestation, work, undertaking, and fulfilment also involves a struggle with numinous powers. In Homer's poetry the empirical and the numinous are blended in a unity of existence, and wherever you have a situation reaching its peak point or an enterprise its maturity you have a numinous presence, and a man's attitude to the first is also his reaction towards the second and thus it receives a certain aura of piety.[15] It may seem at times as though destiny itself were anxious to be compelled and can grant its final favours only as the result of such compulsion. The heroic quality appears to consist, at least partially, in a correspondence to this demand of destiny. There is a hint of this in the recurring theme of legend and fairy tale that something is waiting for liberation, and appealing to the man who can liberate it, and eventually the hero does liberate it by challenging the fearful circumstances by which it is surrounded. And then, but only then, it yields to its liberator.

A man may make the attempt to reach that deeper level where destiny comes into being. It may be through his inner self when he clarifies his mind, purifies his motives, and strengthens his character or, to speak rather in terms of this experience, when he rids himself of what offends or opposes such external forces and adapts himself structurally to them. He can seek protection in religious ideas, forms, and symbols until his inner being is informed and directed by them. He may search for wisdom, reverence, a discipline of desires and self-assertion, and thus secure a harmony with the ultimate laws of Being. The way towards this harmony is revealed in oracles that rest upon genuine religious experience and wisdom. But he may also concentrate on the forces of destiny themselves. He may respect and appeal to them, entreat their good favour, and moderate them by purification and appeasement. He may try to influence them by using magical methods and taking note of favourable and unfavourable times, places and situations, signs and portents

15. Cf. Walter Otto, *The Homeric Gods* (New York, 1954), pp. 223ff.

till we arrive at the different forms of superstition. The essential here is that a man does things which his day-to-day conscience recognizes to be senseless, because his unconscious self is still living in a long-outdated condition and he clings to the magical meaning of such activity.

Fatalism, Stoicism, and Humour

On the other hand, a man may become a fatalist. This indicates nothing more at times than discouragement or weakness. The will capitulates in the face of the overwhelming and unintelligible; that is the end of everything. But it may also indicate a peculiar kind of strength and an opportunity not merely to advance in life but to gain the mastery over it. In this case, a man detaches himself from individual efforts to realize his will and abandons resistance; a harmony is achieved between himself and destiny and he is borne along by it. In psychological terms, he is released from the constraint involved in self-assertion, from the short-sighted attempt to justify himself and the anxiety that attends upon planning for the future. In their stead we discover a readiness to accept whatever will happen, a sensitiveness to the way events develop, which facilitates his capacity for right action.

Such an attitude is foreign to Western man, with his marked leaning towards personal self-assertion and responsibility, but it would appear to be basic in the Eastern technique of life. It has been cultivated with special assiduity in Islam and its spiritual, political, and commercial achievements indicate that this submission to Kismet need not necessarily weaken the forces of practical action.

We may compare this outlook, despite all its differences, with the attitude towards destiny of Northern man in earlier centuries. Northern man believed that everything was spun and measured by the Norns and was fulfilled irrevocably. If we study this attitude as revealed in ancient texts we receive the impression that the primitive Northern

man fundamentally did not have the will to guide the process of events.
158 Behind his immense energy in action and combat, seen in detail, there lies a peculiar passiveness that becomes an instrument of destiny. This is confirmed by the feeling for portents, the premonition of coming events, and that special second sight of primitive Northern life, along with melancholy in its various forms. But as has been remarked, this interior passivity is the core of a mighty will to venture, act, and fight. Indeed, so powerful is this will that, once it has been brought to the pitch of resolution, it can scarcely be altered even by the man who made the resolution. This mood finds its frequent expression in the calamitous oaths to which men pledged themselves over their drinking horns or the commitments they undertook under more and more binding obligations. Perhaps this very force of will is, in the final resort, a kind of helplessness and thus another manifestation of interior passivity. It is tempting to interpret this as an affinity between natural vigour and destiny and as indicating what is often known as the tragic ethos of that period.

A man like this believes that everything occurs as it is ordained, yet in spite of that, he engages his whole energy in carrying through his own projects. He may observe that the course of destiny is unfavourable and none the less fight his way forward with fierce determination. When his plans are wrecked and final defeat draws nigh, his attitude towards the inevitable combines an awareness of the impossibility of success with a firm persistence in his own will. It is an active, tragic fatalism, in which the defeat of a man holding fast to his original purposes is seen as a supreme form of self-fulfilment.[16]

---

16. Perhaps the most complete example of this attitude is found in the figure of the hapless Grettir, pursued by a hostile destiny from the moment of his fight with his enemy, Glam, when he gazed into the fading eyes of the dying man. From then onwards everything is against him; yet he does not withdraw a single step and realizes his grim greatness in his unyielding defeat. Cf. the work, already quoted, *Geschichte von dem starken Grettir*, ed. P. Herrmann.

This tragic fatalism receives further emphasis from the idea that a man must give an emphatic assent to destiny in all its forms, even the most cruel, on the grounds that it is always "life"—in the "amor fati" of Nietzsche which meets whatever happens not only with resignation in the sentence, "I accept this," but with the joyous welcome of "I love this."

A man may, however, regard destiny as essentially alien and hostile and search for an ultimate and unassailable fortress in which he can find a secure foothold. This is the position of the Stoic. He can discover no benevolent pattern in existence and sees no possibility of making it intelligible. Consequently, he jettisons all that can be affected and destroyed by destiny and reserves merely his own self as the last stronghold that cannot be overwhelmed. Everything else, be it property, reputation, health, human relationships, and even life itself, he regards as not properly belonging to himself, he accustoms himself to their loss, and exercises himself in renunciation. For him reality shrinks to an objective focus, the sole function of which is to constitute his self and to remain unshattered when all else has been lost. At this centre the Stoic stands firm and undismayed.

To this negative aspect of ataraxia there corresponds a positive aspect which also is a field for Stoic moral effort: to wit, a mood of growing interior assurance in which he discovers a greater unity and contentment within himself. This self-unity, pure and all-sufficient, may well include an austere but intense mystical experience, when it is felt as the inner centre of existence itself and as transcending destiny. The Stoic technique of living seems to be based upon insensitiveness but this may possibly be an incorrect interpretation. For it confuses the genuine Stoic with a different kind of man only too ready to claim affinity with Stoicism, the moralist whose attitude is dictated wholly by reason and will, a man as firm in principle as he is deficient in affective qualities and who renounces the fulness of experience because he is without feeling. The genuine Stoic, on the other hand, is a very sensitive person, continually bruised in his contact with things and seeking some defensive armour against them: an unwarlike character that feels himself constantly assailed and that abandons the objective of such attack, namely, the concrete goods of this life. It is therefore no accident that the Stoic attitude makes its appearance in periods of disintegration, whether in antiquity or the Middle Ages or in our present age.

Humour provides man with another method of dealing with destiny. The man who has this gift makes no attempt to alter destiny but recognizes it for what it is, with all its hardness, its odd features and contradictions. He understands whatever he can of it and he succeeds in understanding a good deal and suspects that there lurks a concealed meaning in what lies beyond his comprehension. He takes a delight in its extraordinary and queer manifestations, not only because they are original and interesting but also because they confirm the contradictory elements in his own being. He longs for an orderly and harmonious world, but if such a world were provided he would not be able to put up with it. Consequently, he accepts its contradictions and the apparent absence of meaning and, further, he creates a special place for them where they can belong, and so he manages to find a stable position for himself. He is therefore able to transcend the world process and his own existence in an ineffable realm of peace.

The man with a gift of humour puts trust in destiny but is not surprised when things turn out differently, not from any cynical motive but because his broadly based experience tells him that this is in fact what does happen. He suffers, at times very deeply, but he succeeds in avoiding bitterness and meeting life with smiles which, like genuine tears, are a final form of human expression. They contain strength, independence, wisdom, and the patience that never fails. They also include love, love for existence as it is, so that we are tempted to ask whether such humour is possible apart from Redemption: not the clever wit that springs from a heart poor in qualities of loving or is a weapon in the conflict of life; certainly not that grim scorn that sees stupidity and terror in existence and is the breeding ground of contempt and despair; and again, not irony, product of an embarrassed Idealism: no, but genuine humour with its liberty and love, its pain and yet its hidden capacity for enjoyment. It may well be that this kind of humour can exist only in the sphere created by Redemption.

Destiny as Task

We must finally consider another attempt to master destiny by recognizing in it a structure and responsibility with its possibilities and limitations. This approach treats destiny with a blend of confidence and caution; it mingles bold venture with quiet self-possession. It rests upon the moral force of character, on a feeling for reality and moderation, an alertness and sense of duty, but it may all too easily become positivist, narrow, and chilly. It would seem to have been the Roman ethos *par excellence.*

This state of mind searches for the intention of destiny, to understand the challenge of existence to man in the concrete situation. This knowledge is built up of various elements: a sober assessment of the reality in question; an insight into the sources of activity and creation; a feeling for the capacity of the historical process to absorb the action; attention to signs and indications, deterring or encouraging circumstances from which one can learn whether the hour is an open or a closed one, favourable or unfavourable. It needs particularly the gift of assessing and defining the fluidity of the situation, of taking a resolute stand within it, with the courage to tackle it and the strength to accept its consequences. It can be fulfilled only in a final mood of reverence, and this is what really constitutes the reverent spirit of ancient Rome. It may assume very primitive forms but it can also develop to a high pitch of spiritual outlook with a splendid capacity for making history. Vergil's *Aeneid* is its most perfect expression.

But it is wanting in imagination and uplift of heart. In consequence, its realism can readily degenerate till it becomes mere attachment to the data of experience; its practical note may lose warmth and affection and its exactness become pure matter of fact.

These different attempts to conquer destiny—and there are others also[17]—depend upon the relation of basic patterns of life to existence and they occur continually in man's experience. They include a possible

---

17. A brief reference needs to be made to the unparalleled use of the notion of destiny in Germany during the twelve years of Nazi leadership. In theory, it was linked with the Germanic notion of destiny, on the one side, and, on the other, with the tragic this-worldly concept of Nietzsche. Pedagogy did its best to educate youth in a readiness to embrace destiny. Poetry presented the picture of the heroic man filled with an awareness of his destiny. In public speeches, the press, and the general interpretation of life a Germanic mentality, inspired by the force of destiny and of bravery in the face of destiny, was lauded as a counterbalance to Jewish calculation and Christian tender-heartedness. Enthusiastic because of the splendour of the "Reich," the new man must feel he is summoned to encounter danger and the threat of death and to rise to loftier planes of being through this willingness to meet destiny.

This trend of thought was honourably intended by a number of idealists but for the great majority it was so much idle talk. The authorities used it, however, as a means to persuade the youth and the people generally to respond to their every mood and dispensation. The closing years of the war, and especially its final outcome, showed only too clearly how appallingly they had succeeded. Things reached such a pass that not only a political sense but even the simplest human sanity would have made them give up in order to preserve the residue of life, property, and cultural heritage that still remained, for future reconstruction. Instead, the "leaders" harried the people at their mercy to quite literal extinction. This presupposed on the part of the people a long-established absence of judgment and resolution which had ended by becoming a collective psychosis. Had there been any doubt about the motives of the leaders it was entirely dispelled by the eventual outcome. When the time came not only to entrust others to destiny but to take a stand against it themselves, they displayed a shamelessness without parallel. Anyone who was not wilfully blinding himself could see that the whole belief in "destiny" had been nothing but a tool of a cynical will to power.

method for dealing with destiny. In periods of good fortune and power, of confidence or interior serenity, this gives the impression of succeeding but on the whole it is a failure. All that is left of it in concrete life is resignation, the sense that it is impossible to find a way out or to discover any meaning.

DESTINY AND REVELATION

The Transformation of This Experience of Destiny in Faith

This experience of destiny assumed a different form in periods of mythology and in rationalist ages, in North and South, among peasants in the country and townsmen in cities. But there is a common trait that persists throughout, namely, an awareness of some exterior circumstance that determines existence and yet itself is beyond all human influence, and which in the last resort is not to be assessed by the known standards of measure, right and good.

Man's prospects of mastering or even enduring it are found within its sphere of action as a greater or smaller share in good fortune, power, health, serenity, and toughness: against destiny itself he can avail nothing. He can neither penetrate the pattern of destiny nor bring pressure to bear upon its powers: not merely because it would be too hidden or too powerful but also because, as a numinous factor, it transcends all effective approach. Now, it is true that man also has a numinous centre

---

Experience, however, should open men's eyes to the consequences of this enthronement of so many pagan values, whether they derived from Germanic tradition or from antiquity. The theories give the impression of being profound, the programme is extensive, its criticism of Christianity runs along glibly, and a growing number of people willingly accept it. Closer scrutiny reveals its ultimate motives, which are neither profound nor well put together, and history, as it unfolds, shows what destruction has been wrought by them.

from which, once he has actuated it, he can enter into a real relation with the hidden forces of destiny and attempt to influence them through feeling and concentration, through cultus and magic. But again, in the last instance, he does not come into contact with it, since it remains concealed behind the empirical, metaphysical, and numinous forms that he can discover.

Destiny is something *impersonal*; it is the impersonal *par excellence.* When a man speaks indeliberately of "it," he is referring to destiny and to his own commitment to its power which, when everything is considered, knows neither justice nor wisdom, neither reverence nor goodness, but seems to provide a ground for what is cold and indifferent and meaningless, and even for evil. The sense of destiny weighs like a dull burden upon the spirit. It is the interior focus of human melancholy.

Within the sphere of revelation destiny, as thus envisaged, does not exist. No sooner does Christian faith become dominant in men's lives than the sense of destiny is transformed. How this happens must be discovered in the source of revelation, in the person of Jesus.

Destiny in the Life of Jesus

Let us look at the pattern of Jesus' life in its details. His descent from a royal house in decline and His very modest social and economic situation; the thirty years of youth and manhood spent in hidden retirement with the tensions arising from them; His awe-inspiring sense of responsibility as Messias and the intense awareness of Himself as Redeemer; the consciousness that He is to fulfil and at the same time transform all previous history; the special character of His knowledge, not only wide and profound but capable of grasping, penetrating, and judging the nature of existence itself; the unerring clarity of absolute standards and the immense force of His character; the power of His Being and will, before which apparently nothing is impossible. All this reveals the particular pattern of His life: how He is ringed with loneliness, with no companions at His own level, so that His intimate circle of disciples misunderstand Him no less than the general crowd; how persons in authority and responsible positions misunderstand, depreciate, and calumniate Him and set the uncritical mob against Him; how all His love and self-communication, all His assistance and generosity are of no avail till in the end, after at most three years, His activity ceases with accusation and trial, and the terrible death upon the cross. If we reflect on all this, we may well conclude that Jesus was filled with a most oppressive sense of destiny.

A closer examination confirms this impression. Jesus is bound by all the necessities of existence, which are all the harder because of the very restricted circumstances in which He lives. He wields, it is true, a formidable power. This is shown in the radiance of His personality, His mastery over Nature, the assurance with which He reads into the hearts of men, the force of Divine truth and love and the spiritual vigour of His teaching. The accounts in the Gospels show us again and again the strong impression made by this. But it is an essential part of His attitude that He never employs it to break through the barriers that have been imposed on Him. This must have given rise to an intense feeling of being confined, and in effect this is taken for granted in the temptation at the beginning of His public career when Satan tempts Him to break out of the limits imposed (Matt. 4:1–11).

The position is still further complicated by events that have accumulated through a history of many centuries, a history rich with emotion, struggle, injustice, and disaster: all the rebellion against God's leadership, the many complications and tensions that have developed and achieved their final outlet in Jesus. Since the Babylonian exile concepts and judgments, attitudes of will and sentiment have hardened round the person and mission of the Messias and in consequence every expression of His

Being, every sentence of His teaching is caught up in them. How hard these fetters are is seen in the repeated reproaches of Jesus against His own people and His sympathy, an almost nostalgic sympathy, for the heathen (Matt. 11:16–24; 22:15–19; 14:10–12, etc.). This is heightened by the untrustworthiness of His followers, their inability to comprehend, their narrowness and weakness, and finally the fact that one of His most intimate circle betrayed Him (Matt. 16:6–11; Luke 18:31–34; Acts 1:6–7, etc.). Throughout it all, humanly speaking, runs a disturbing strain that is haphazard and meaningless. If only there had been one loyal and courageous man among the disciples, able to canalize the good dispositions of the people and persuade it to pass a favourable verdict! Could not Pilate, who clearly understood the situation, was moved by Jesus' personality, and had the authority to act, have used this authority in the interests of justice! The tone of the whole situation is manifest in the abominable farce at Herod's court, the "friendship" concluded between Herod and Pilate, and the mockery heaped upon Jesus by the soldiery. And Jesus evidently recognizes, amid these human and historical factors that determine the situation, another lurking factor, the "power of darkness," operating its own hidden evil (Luke 22:53 and John 15:30; for its wider operation, Luke 4:1–13, especially the final verse).

Behind it all, however, there is the special centre of His Being, the Incarnation of the Son of God, which after the creation of the world is "the fact" in the fullest sense of that word. The former is the foundation of Being, the latter establishes the meaning and order of history. This fact means more than that Jesus Christ, like any other man, existed under certain historical and social circumstances; it means that He confined the Divine sovereignty of His Person within the limits of human nature. The essence of this is expressed in one sentence of Paul's Epistle to the Philippians: "Let this mind be in you, which was also in Christ Jesus: who being in the form of God, thought it not robbery to be equal with

God (yet man hangs on to this so anxiously) but emptied Himself, taking the form of a servant, being made in the likeness of men, and in habit found as a man" (2:5–7).

We cannot discuss here the situation resulting from this. It would take us into the ultimate problems of Jesus' mode of existence.[18] But one thing is quite certain, namely, that from it, humanly speaking, must have developed a frightening sense of being shut in and confined. These various considerations hint at the presence in Jesus of elements making up a most terrible experience of destiny. Jesus knows that what is at stake is the salvation of the world, and nothing less, the beginning of a new creation. Not only does He foretell, insist upon, and demand His hour with its immeasurable possibilities; He brings it on with full authority. That "immense design of God" in which everything is to be fulfilled, the "kingdom of God," could "arrive" in its historical course. But, because it consists in God's sovereignty over persons in truth and justice, it must be freely accepted by these persons and it thus depends upon their decision. The persons who make this decision are, for what they are, the people of the time, in Nazareth, Capharnaum, and Jerusalem. In consequence, this divine possibility is submerged beneath an incomprehensible mound of narrowness, cowardice, stupidity, touchiness, jealousy, and vileness.[19] What actually happens is terrible, revolting, disgusting to the last degree, and therefore destiny of the most terrible sort. But is it really "destiny"? Does Jesus experience it as "destiny"?

The answer to this question will differ according as we leave the existence of Jesus free in its own unique character or fit it into categories that are inapplicable: for instance, that of the genius who founders because

18. I hope to say something on this problem in a general synthesis of the content of Christian revelation.

19. Cf. Guardini, *The Lord* (1954), pp. 208ff.

of the narrow circumstances in which he is placed, or the religious hero whose failure is the final proof of his genuineness, or in some other tragic guise. It is tempting to do this for it provides a facile solution. But this solution is specious and in point of fact the whole meaning is lost. To do justice to the existence of Jesus you must let it manifest itself for what it is and draw your ideas from it. Once this is done, it is evident that there was no sense of destiny in the consciousness of Jesus. What happened was certainly experienced by Him with great severity, as witness the hour in Gethsemane; but how exactly He experienced it, it is difficult to say and we shall need many distinctions and nuances to provide anything like an adequate conception.

What happens to Jesus is unnatural, painful, destructive, yet it is not alien but in a curious way familiar to Him. Right to the end He does all He can, in the spirit of His mission, to bring things to a right conclusion, but we have no impression of a special conflict with its tension, its ebb and flow, its possible victory or defeat. Nor can one say that He passively allows events to overwhelm Him; He lets them approach and then takes them to His own heart, but not as if He—in the sense of *amor fati*—decided to assent even to the most terrifying fate. It is rather as though everything is gathered into a personal relationship, and here we approach what is in Him unique.

This transforms the character of events. The force that is operating is no "power," no metaphysical or mythical "something," but always and entirely a person: the person, in the complete sense, with whom Jesus is most intimately connected, the Father; not "the Father of gods and men," not one of the father-deities found in a whole series of religions, but "His Father," so entirely and exclusively His that He associates no man, however dear to Him, with this relationship. Here He stands alone. This relationship is unique. All relations between man and man, even those of a religious man to an historically known God or deity, are included within the sphere of existence. Even the relation to "the Father of gods and men" or to the "Supreme Unity" is within the compass of universal Being. This is not the case—and absolutely not the case—with the relation of Jesus to His Father, for He is the Eternal Son. It is rather the Absolute that for its own part embraces the world. Jesus' consciousness is not that of a man stirred to an extraordinary association with God in the course of history; it comprehends history, it embraces the world. Whatever exists lies within His Divine-human consciousness and His relation to the Father that fulfils it. John is speaking of this relation when he says that Jesus is the eternal Word of the Father "through which everything was made...that was made" (1:3).[20] With this Father Jesus' relation is that of one who is sent and is obedient: not like a creature whose insight and judgment lie outside God's designing mind, but on a plane of equality which is sharply emphasized (John 8:25–30, 42–47, 54–59 etc.). Judged as obedience, His filial obedience is as Divine as is the command of His Father, in terms of command.[21]

A fundamental harmony exists between Jesus and the Father. It finds expression in various statements that His will and that of the Father are one (John 4:35; 5:19–30; 6:38, among others). The objective of this harmony is the kingdom of God, the re-creation of man and the world through grace. The form in which this harmony is actualized is love, the

---

20. This is not extraneous metaphysics or mythology. The apostle is pointing to something he has "observed" in Jesus: the essential basis of His personality. This interpretation is foreshadowed in the other evangelists, e.g., in Luke's sentence: "All things are delivered to me by my Father, and no one knoweth who the Son is but the Father; and who the Father is but the Son and he to whom the Son will reveal Him" (10:22); in the teaching on the Eucharist (Matt. 26:26–28) and in other texts. Cf. Guardini, *Das Wesen des Christentums* (1939), pp. 68ff.

21. The obedience of Jesus Christ belongs not merely to His humanity but also to His Divine person. This is always stressed when we read of the sending of the Son through the Father: frequently in John, and very markedly also in the Epistle to the Hebrews, 10:5–7. This obedience denotes something within divinity, belonging to God's own life.

love existing between Christ and the Father and which subsequently, as
170 the love of the Redeemer, is directed towards man and the world (John 6:40, 47–58, etc.). All that happens to Christ is assumed into this love. Whatever enters into His life, be it necessity or actual fact or, in the sense outlined above, chance, is part of the historical development of that Father-Son relationship. The very way in which the course of events is made concrete in the situation provides the form in which the Father's love is made manifest and it determines the conditions in which the love of the only-begotten Son makes its response. Jesus has His own manner of indicating this; He calls it "His hour" (John 4:2, etc.). Its content is, in the first place, what has been determined in our analysis of destiny. But in Jesus' consciousness its character has been completely transformed and it has become what His Father will have from Him, what He will do in obedience to His Father, and what is willed by Father and Son in the absolute harmony of love.

At this point we should have to consider the moral outlook of Jesus—for example, how He stands with regard to good and evil, what are the motives of His action, and how this motivation works. We should also need to inquire how the predominant acts of mental and spiritual life proceed from Him—knowledge, the assessment of values, choice and action—and what is the structure of His affective life. With this a subsidiary question would be connected, namely, the relation of His unconscious to His conscious life, or, more fundamentally, whether He had an unconscious life, in the ordinary meaning of the term, or maybe there was something very different in its place, and how this ought to be conceived. Finally, we should have to speak of the character of His existence and its difference from our existence as well as His relation to life and death. In a word, the problem of Jesus' psychology would call for analysis—the most difficult task for a psychologist, and the only answer might well be that it is insoluble. All these problems would have their relevance to our present subject but here they must remain untouched.[22]

As regards the problem of destiny, we can at least insist that there is evidently nothing evil in Jesus. He declared this Himself (John 8:46) and it is confirmed by a careful study of His character, His action, and His life. His innocence goes to the very roots of His Being and His orientation towards good, to His Father's will, is absolute. Further, His attitude towards good is unique. For Him it is no imperative, appealing to His will and imposing an obligation upon it. He is found, so to say, on the side of good right from the start. He appears in His earthly existence as the messenger of good and He challenges "man" as its champion: and this, not as an ordinary prophet, himself subject to the demands of good and found wanting in God's sacred judgment, yet still representing its claims upon men. He does so essentially and in His very nature. There are two solemn occasions, the baptism in the Jordan and the transfiguration upon the mountain, when the Father declares: "This is my well beloved Son, in whom I am well pleased" (Matt. 3:17; 17:5). This Divine pleasure does not derive from a past perseverance in good, as God declares in the case of Moses (Num. 12:7); it belongs to a far more fundamental order and is identical with the fact that Jesus is the Son of the Father. When John says that Jesus is the Logos, the manifestation of the hidden Father in the openness of truth and at the same time the "light of men," the condition of the truth of Being and knowledge for everything created (John 1:1–5), it is equally true to say that He is the manifestation of the Father in the right and glory of the good and also the norm of action for mankind: the master of "discipleship" and the judge of everything upon earth (Matt. 10:32–39; 23:31–46).[23]

---

22. I hope to discuss these matters in the general synthesis of revelation previously noted.
23. Guardini, *Des Wesen des Christentums*, pp. 67ff., 73ff.

In Christ, then, there is nothing of that interior confusion discussed in our analysis of destiny, no contradiction between one tendency and another, between unconscious and conscious life; to that essential harmony with the Father He brings a Being, wholly flawless and unified.

The psychology of the acts that create His immediate field of action is, like that of His interior life, quite unique. Undoubtedly, in His case too, a large number of elements were chosen and fitted together to form a milieu peculiar to Himself, conditioned by all the elements that contributed to His reality in the concrete—family, people, country, point of historical development, and others. Yet this selection obviously does not touch the ground of His existence. This is to be discovered, unaffected, within His sphere of life, and to it He has a direct and comprehensive relation. It is impossible to put Jesus into any category of human existence—that of warrior, artist, scientist, philosopher, politician, social worker, or even teacher, and not even founder of a religion. On the contrary, He is "man" in an absolute sense and "manifestation of God," truly the "Son of man," a title He so frequently applied to Himself. From this derives His power to realize a perfect encounter with every man. This does not mean that He discusses scientific questions with a scientist or talks about affairs of State with a politician. The question often raised as to whether He could do this and whether He possesses the requisite knowledge and so forth is entirely beside the point. What Jesus certainly can do is to appeal to the full humanity of every man through all differences of individuality and status and to bring him into association with God. His immediate world is therefore poised in a balance all its own, a balance between a precise determination which limits Him to a particular point in the world and in history and a universality which identifies His immediate world with existence as a whole.

In consequence, His every experience remains completely open. What will happen to Jesus is never determined by His nature or mission or by the situation in which He is.[24] We can never conclude from the external pressure or the interior forces in some event that things had to occur as they did. That would leave us with glib tragedy or a misconceived popular fatalism.[25] Everything could have happened otherwise. Pilate might have done his duty. Even at the moment of the crucifixion one of those in high authority might have reflected and called a halt to the ghastly affair. Jesus did not create a pattern of destiny for Himself through character and action; still less did an unconscious will of self-punishment and self-destruction produce a doom. In effect, Jesus faces the entire range of possibility in existence and accepts what is prepared for Him by natural laws, by the structure of social life and the decisions of individual men.

The fundamental attitude of Jesus' life develops in this atmosphere of openness: His readiness to accept and accomplish what the hour brings, His obedience to the Father's will. Further, within Him is a power that helps the decisive moment of history to unroll itself. He does not prevent men from becoming what they wish to become; He does not silence them or direct or outmanoeuvre them. His approach brings men fundamentally to Himself in their true Being and He further encourages them to reveal their true selves. A man is determined by the attitude he adopts towards Christ. The real effect of Redemption is to make this clear; it is at once liberation and judgment. The strength with which Jesus puts this truth into effect is identical with His obedience, which

24. This also follows from an analysis of the life pattern of Jesus in distinction from those of prominent historical figures. He is purely and simply "Himself": in fact, it is doubtful whether we ought to speak of a "pattern" for His life as we do in the case of the Buddha, Socrates, and the like.

25. The sentence, "Ought not Christ to have suffered these things, and so to enter into His glory?" (Luke 24:26), does not signify any historical necessity or pressure of destiny. It can be understood only in terms of God's design which links freedom and necessity and in the final resort remains inscrutable.

accepts the course of events as they develop. In fact, He is called at a decisive moment, "a sign which shall be contradicted," "set for the fall and the resurrection of many" (Luke 2:34).

This makes it clear how impossible it is to fit Jesus' existence into the psychological schema of existence as influenced by destiny. His relation to the Father and, as a consequence of this, His relation to the world are of an altogether different kind.

In this relation there disappears the alien, chilly and oppressive note that is characteristic of destiny. There is an atmosphere of intimacy; everything is an expression of love. The word has no idyllic or sentimental meaning. Its significance is stronger and, in a Divine sense, harder than any mythology of heroic existence. Its content is the Father's commission to Christ, Himself to experience the terrible reality of the fallen world, to redeem it and "so enter into His glory" (Luke 24:26).

The mysterious element in destiny which may at times seem an absence or even denial of meaning vanishes in this harmony. That, in purely human terms, what happened must have appeared mysterious is shown by words like those spoken at Gethsemane: "If it be possible, let this chalice pass from me," and on the cross: "My God, why hast Thou forsaken me?" (Matt. 26:23 and 27:46). Yet these words are linked with that perfect harmony. They do not remove, we repeat, the Divine hardness of Jesus' life, for it is Redemption that is at stake, which means that Jesus is experiencing in perfect truth and liberty the condition of the world. The fearful element is none the less there, as is proved by these words that express the fear of created Being. To endure it calls for the highest degree of sincerity, an inflexibility of resolution, loyalty and fearlessness and strength and much besides. Nevertheless, what happens is caught up in an absolute significance of love, which Jesus understands, and in which no question is left unresolved. On the contrary, the absolute truth and power of Redemption are possible only because they proceed from this love. Only such a love can engender such a truth.

In Jesus' relation to the Father there vanishes also that sense of blind compulsion against which mankind employs its many devices to alter, deviate, and outmanoeuvre it, only to realize in the end that it has no alternative but to yield to it or to work out its doom in heroic tragedy. Of this there is no question in Jesus. His will does not feel subject to the power that disposes of Him; it is within it. For this power is the Father's will, not acting with alien pressure but united with His own will in understanding and vivid resolution, as is continually made clear by John. The words already quoted from Gethsemane and Golgotha point, it is true, to a distinction and an opposition that indicate there is no monistic coalescence, and the actual circumstances of destiny remain as they were. But in both instances the succeeding sentences show how perfectly the will of Jesus is one with that of the Father: "Not my will but Thine be done" and "Into Thy hands I commend my spirit" (Luke 22:42; 23:46). The Father's command and Jesus' obedience are linked at the root of that whole process which otherwise would be destiny but which here is something entirely different, namely, harmony in redeeming love.

The numinous factor in destiny that confronts man as impenetrable mystery and sustains and favours or disturbs or compels or crushes or even overmasters him with a demonic horror, making him despair completely of salvation—this, too, is transformed in Jesus. The mystery continues. The realm of God's design and of the prevailing power of spirit permeates all words and actions. But it is holy, not merely in a general sense but in the personal, moral sense of pure responsibility, of absolute truth and goodness, of perfect understanding and act. The vague numinous cloud that according to its advocates ranges from "physical

shudder" and "ghostly horror" to "adoration" is lifted and clarified, and
176 there is shown forth the mystery of the living God.[26]

One factor that plays a significant rôle in Jesus' life and yet may confuse the modern reader is the hostility of Satan. It calls for closer inquiry.[27]

One might be tempted to dismiss the whole notion as conditioned by the peculiar views of that age. Yet Jesus' awareness of being opposed to Satan and his kingdom cannot be taken out of the context of His knowledge of His mission. This is evident from many passages, especially the accounts of cures. The form these frequently take is the expulsion by Jesus of a demon that is the active cause of the disease. Here, there can be no question of primitive ideas; it is quite impossible that in a matter of such religious importance Jesus can have accepted false notions from His own age. When He addresses Satan behind the illnesses, revelation means that Satan is actually there. The statement is not a medical diagnosis, it concerns the condition of the world, to wit, that it is in the power of Satan.[28] Satan says, as he tempts Him: "To Thee will I give all this power (over the riches of the world and its glory)" and he adds: "for to me they are delivered, and to whom I will, I give them" (Luke 4:6). Jesus does not contradict his claim but raises the holy sovereignty of His Father above the dominion of evil. At His capture He says to His enemies: "This is your hour and the power of darkness" (Luke 22:53), and He significantly employs that expression "the hour" which he uses

26. Cf. G. V. d. Leeuw, *Phänomenologie der Religion*, p. 29; also, at an earlier date, Rudolf Otto, *Das Heilige* (1932), pp. 16ff.

27. The subject is very complicated and mysterious and here a preliminary answer must suffice. But see also Guardini, *The Lord*, pp. 115ff., and *Der Widersacher*, in the series *Christliche Besinnung*, No. 37 (1940).

28. The statement of Jesus at the raising of Lazarus is most illuminating: ἐνεβριμήσατο τῷ πνεύματι. This does not mean, as has been often suggested, that "He shuddered" but that "He grew angry in spirit." Jesus is touched with Divine anger at the indignity which holds the world a prisoner and has now smitten his friend.

to indicate the Father's will as it continually reveals itself. Elsewhere He refers to Satan as "the prince of this world" who has no hold upon Him (John 14:30; also 16:11) and He speaks of a Satanic kingdom, an evil order of things and relationships (Matt. 12:26). Jesus thus declares that Satan possesses a real power in the world, a dominion over men and things. He is not, as Dualists urge, an evil principle who constructed the world together with the good principle but a creature of God, originally good but who in sinning became evil. In his own right he would possess no power at all and he must, for instance, "desire" to "sift the disciples as wheat" (Luke 22:31). But this power has been granted to him as a consequence and punishment of the original sin, in which man refused obedience to God.

This power is everywhere operative. It conceals itself behind good in the world, and even behind the numinous factor within it. Paul goes so far as to consider the gods to be demons (1 Cor. 11:21) and his opinion is shared by the early Christians.[29] Thus Satan is a ruler of a "kingdom" that permeates the whole of existence and influences all behaviour. This means, in terms of our present problem, that he is active at the very source of destiny. The element of malice, evil, and coldness we have mentioned is his will. Its intention is to dethrone God, to construct a world that no longer belongs to God. To start with, he tempts man to concentrate on himself, to transfer his allegiance to himself (cf. Gen. 3:1–5). But man cannot in truth do this since he has an essential orientation to a unique and absolute Being. His truth is found in "service," taking the word in its noblest meaning. The proclamation of man's autonomy can therefore represent only a transitional moment. If man deserts his true

29. This view may be sometimes expressed in too devastating a way, and in any case it needs to be studied in detail. There is much wisdom and beauty in the presentation of the ancient deities but they do keep man enclosed completely in the world and are thus figures that falsify and mislead.

Lord, "whom to serve is to reign,"[30] then he falls a victim to the arch-rebel, whose service is slavery and shame.

Jesus broke this evil dominion. The Gospels depict His life as filled with a "conflict," concerned only to a small extent with empirical enemies: far more importantly—and to Jesus this is the sole importance—it is waged against Satan and his kingdom. The conflict does not consist in concentration of will or the employment of magical forces but in the Divine purity of Jesus, on which temptations can lay no hold, in the sacred truth of His message, in His unerring faithfulness to the prescription of His Father's will even though it led Him through straits and self-abnegation, through humiliation and suffering, to a terrible death; in His redeeming assumption of the world's guilt before the Father's justice, which entailed suffering of a cruelty beyond measure; and finally, in the events of the last days and the death on the cross which, together with the Resurrection, is recognized from the beginning as "the victory," "the triumph." Yet, fundamentally, what is taking place all the time is not a struggle but a "judgment," as John explicitly declares: "Now is the judgment of the world. Now shall the prince of this world be cast out" (12:31; also 16:11).

It is not easy to make up our minds how we must envisage this judgment. To begin with, Jesus has compelled Satan to emerge into the light. Previously he was in the "darkness," hidden behind objects and events in the world that had been shut against God (1 John 5:10–11). The very figures of demonology had served as screens since their number and their lack of religious and cultural value showed inevitably how false they were. The holiness and truth of the God-man made clear the deceit of the arch-rebel and his basic evil and uncleanness. The eye that has been blest with the freedom of faith can now recognize him and what is

30. Cf. Mass *pro pace*, Post-Communion.

his. In the second place, it is obvious that Satan's relation to the world has been considerably altered. Despite the ferocity of the "power of darkness" unleashed against Him, Jesus remained in the Father's will and thus made atonement for men's sins. From that point onwards, Satan has no further direct power over things; and only so much over men as they give him because of their disposition or, correspondingly, what God permits for the working out of sacred history. He is now only one force among the other forces in the world, though one no doubt of immense range and alarming subtlety. The Apocalypse lets us see how seriously he is assessed in revelation. Christ's word, however, stands guarantor that the believer, who entrusts himself to faith, is held firm and secure in Redemption.

To conclude: the manner in which events enter into the life of Jesus and are experienced by Him is not "destiny" in any of its normal meanings. It seems impossible to find a positive name for it, since this would suppose a full understanding of His mind.

It acquires a proper name only when the believer participates in it; then it is known as providence.[31]

Destiny and Providence

We have been considering the form of existence that belongs essentially to Jesus Christ. It could be fulfilled only by Him, for it presupposes this special and exclusive relation to the Father.

But He has this existence not only for Himself but also in His quality of Redeemer. It is not "private" but in an absolute sense "public." Jesus was essentially "sent," lived His life so that every man, given vision and encouragement through Him, can now realize that existence in the nature of things but He has established it through His action. His

31. This is dealt with more fully later in pp. 186ff.

life and action form the beginning of a new existence. To be redeemed means to enter into Him through the grace of this beginning and to live from Him.

The basic acts of this existence are faith, hope, and love. Faith commences with Christ as the absolute beginning, and since it cannot fix itself in a this-worldly pattern, it can be realized increasingly only in a stable, personal abiding-in-Christ (cf. John 15:3–7 and 1 John 2:24–28). Love is personal union with Jesus as the absolute lover and "life for His will, as He doth the will of the Father" (John 6:57). But hope is the certainty that this new beginning, which is contradicted by "the old," the whole condition of the unredeemed world, will be realized in complete richness and stability and will be finally consummated in eternity (Rom. 8:18–25).

How, then, in the light of revelation, are we to consider what has been described hitherto as destiny?

It is the world, the pattern of things, and the course of events in their relation to man who has revolted against God. It is existence as it has developed from original sin and the growing volume of subsequent sin, from those moods and attitudes, those views, tendencies, and circumstances in which sin has solidified itself. This condition of existence was the consequence of sin, that is, punishment inflicted as such by the justice of the Lord of the world.

Man had experience of this in one of its natural consequences, namely, blindness. To man's "narrowed" vision this condition of the world which derived from sin appeared as though it were controlled by destiny. Hence the various notions of powers and spheres of destiny are part of that confusion arising out of sin. Man did not see things as they really are.

Christ was the first to make this clear. The first fruit of Redemption was the unveiling of reality. In this light, it was seen that there is no such thing as destiny as unredeemed man conceived and continues to conceive it but merely a world that has fallen away from God and experiences the results of that apostasy. Gone are the frustration and apprehension and also the self-centredness and the pathos of belief in destiny. Truth shines forth as cleaner and firmer and more comforting. It became evident that the seeming domination of destiny was in reality the dominion of the living God, namely, punishment for sin. Behind this stood Providence. Men were to experience the consequences of sin as a preparation for Redemption.

When Jesus came, the state of the world was transformed. The mere discovery of the true character of destiny indicated a change, for it was no longer possible to speak of the world as men had been doing, except in the form of a new apostasy. At the same time the new commencement was inaugurated: the existence of Jesus in which man could participate by His grace. The whole pattern of existence was fundamentally altered. The same happened and continues to happen now that the world is directed by the Father towards and out from Christ: this is Providence in the proper sense. And finally, this beginning, once established, gave rise and gives rise continually to decisions and attitudes on the believer's part and states and patterns of life that were and are just as real.

Of course, a man can repudiate this relationship. He can choose the world exclusively, without Christ and without the living God. In that case, the old condition of things breaks through once again. Because a man's eyes lose their focus in the measure in which he apostatizes from Christ, the distorted vision sees this state of affairs again as destiny. But this is not precisely the situation; it is in fact much more dangerous. Redemption has raised the world to an absolutely higher plane of values and decisions and it remains there, whether it likes this or not.[32] If man

32. Consequently, once Christ has come, the quality of evil becomes intensified.

rejects the Redemption, then what he calls "destiny" is far more alarming than before.

Once a man believes in Christ, Providence takes the place of destiny in directing his existence. This brings him by means of grace into the relation existing between the Father and the Incarnate Son. The transition is not immediate. Belief in destiny belongs to unredeemed existence and may well be its most profound expression; as the outlook of "the old man" (Eph. 4:22) it continues even in the believer. But within him a process is operative which the New Testament terms "the adoption of sons," the acceptance as children of God (Gal. 4:5). This is no mere feeling of security in God or of trust in Him; it is a new form of existence with the strength to put it into effect. To the degree in which "the old man is put off" and "the new man put on"—and this happens in every genuine act of the Christian life—the notion of destiny is changed into that of Providence.

In place of the mysterious, impersonal force conceived as destiny there appears the person of the Father.

The whole character of existence is now transformed. What occurs to a man becomes an act of responsibility. "Destiny" lacks responsibility. The Parcae and Norns, Moira and Ananke are not answerable for their dispositions. They are unaware of what they doing, for they are not persons but forces, elements in the world. Among the basic truths of revelation is the guarantee that all that happens—if it be permitted to happen—is on God's responsibility. Not that God first willed something and then this had to be right but what He wills and does, He wills and does because it is true and right. Of course, there is no law of true and right suspended above Him so that He is forced to act according to it. He is Himself this law. This does not make His action arbitrary but "obligatory" in a more profound sense than man can be "obliged" by an ethical commandment. God is absolutely "obliged" through Himself and at the same time absolutely free. He is responsible before His own Supreme Dignity—"for His name's sake," as Scripture says (Jer. 14:7 and elsewhere)—that all that occurs is true and right. Naturally, this does not signify that the content of an individual human act must be good, for this depends upon the freedom of the individual man who can will evil as well as good.

Evil and badness are subject, in the last resort, to a final order of judgment, an order already evident in many respects but one that will be wholly revealed in the Judgment. To the extent to which one man's acts affect another man, we have another pledge from the same God in the sentence, that "to those that love God, all things work together unto good," that is, will realize an order of salvation (Rom. 8:28). Judged from this standpoint, belief in destiny is seen in an unwonted light as degradation. The mythology, the metaphysics, and the ethics of destiny interpret it as the special element of grandeur veiled in mystery. In actual fact, it is a degrading force with no conceivable justification. At its centre, behind the veil of mysterious solemnity yawns the abyss of nothingness. A man who has had the vivid experience of seeing it unveiled knows the true meaning of Redemption.

Where formerly man was a prisoner delivered to destiny he is now a man redeemed, whom grace has taken up into communion with the Son of God and His relation with the Father.

Another fundamental truth of revelation applies to the redeemed, to wit, that God not only disposes of him with power or cares for him benevolently but that He also has regard, respect, for him. For man is a person. This is how God willed him, and has established him in an association of dignity with Himself. Therefore, God's relation to man rests everywhere on this respect. This personal dignity remains even in evil. It is what makes evil particularly evil in man and lends his humiliation its characteristic note. This person has respect for God, especially in His

conserving Providence. The very wrath of God, which is no subjective
184
mood of anger but the expression of His living holiness confronted with evil, His very condemnations and punishments, are directed to the person and are thus based upon this respect.

Previously, men felt themselves completely abandoned to destiny; they are now conscious of the near presence of God.

Our immediate concepts of God and our relation to Him have been altered through revelation and in a novel way. It has made it particularly clear that God is not naturally linked with the world and that between Him and the world there lies the abyss of absolute sovereignty. This is why Christianity appears a good deal less "pious" than non-Christian religions. At the same time God has drawn near to the human person: there is no hint of this in purely natural reverence. God is now "with" the believer as one person with another.[33] The creature's isolation is removed in a manner undreamt of in any natural unity or universal coalescence.

Gone now are the indifference and emptiness which belief in destiny saw at the heart of things; in their stead appears the love of the Father.

All that happens derives from this love. There is nothing weak in it, it has nothing to do with that kindness and sentimentality that are ascribed to it. The Father's love is truth, justice, and power. God has established man in genuine Being and set him in a realm of real freedom. He does not use him as means to end but honours him in the dignity of his personality. Indeed, God has drawn man to Himself in a way that transcends

---

33. God's personality is of course unique. The word "person" applies to God absolutely but man is a person only in so far as he has established himself in his own individual being. God is also holy but man is this worldly and, as the result of sin, unholy. It has been God's pleasure to establish man in that relationship to Himself. In fact, man realizes personality only in this relation to God, as one called by God, whom God has drawn to Himself in an I-Thou association. Consequently, God's personality, though it is beyond all comparison, does not exclude or destroy human personality; on the contrary, it is its foundation.

all statement and touches the inner core of revelation. There is no question of natural identification or pantheistic confusion, which for all their seeming profundity disturb the real depths; it is something of which revelation alone can give us assurance. When one man loves another with a personal earnestness, the defensive attitude of "You, not myself" crumbles; what concerns the other now concerns him also. God has willed that a relation of this sort should exist between Himself and man: this is evident from the whole story of revelation and it comes to fulfilment in His Incarnation, wherein He quite literally assumed human existence.[34]

This love is at the centre of God's direction of the world. If we allow the phrase to have its widest meaning, the mainspring of God's direction of the world is God's heart. This states equivalently that "to those that love God, all things work together unto good" (Rom. 8:28). This "good" must not be understood in the sense of mere welfare, as is evident from the most superficial view of life, and not in the further sense of an unfolding of personality and activity, as daily experience shows. Many things are always possible, want, embitterment, and destruction of various kinds to the point of meaninglessness. The "good" is rather the realization of God's proper and permanent conception of man in association with God's kingdom. Good and ill fortune, challenge and development, and also hindrance and destruction may be necessary for this. Only God understands what is the right thing, and therefore belief in Providence takes us back to His judgment that surpasses all comment and to His impenetrable design. But these are wisdom and love. The step taken into the incomprehensible is a positive one: it consists of confident love as an answer to provident love. It is convinced that whatever happens, in its absolute vigour and delicacy, its pure precision and its immense solemnity, corresponds with the exigencies of the sacred process.

---

34. Cf. Guardini, *Welt und Person*, pp. 129ff.; also, *Die christliche Liebe* (1940), pp. 19ff.

 What in the acceptance of destiny was wholly unintelligible now becomes a mystery which, though it may remain insoluble, stirs and secures our confidence.

All events are taken up into the pattern we have been describing. They lose nothing of their gravity and harshness, but they are given a further quality, since the Father's love is behind them, and the believer in Christ has a share in this. At first, things remain as they are, but the believer acquires a new stand and support, a guarantee and a strength, through which the whole of existence is transformed. It is not easy to maintain this and to make it effective since reality does not give the impression that Christ's message is adapted to and fits in with it. As far as impression goes, belief in destiny would seem right, and all the rest a fairy tale. But we have been given revelation, not merely for our consolation but as a task to be fulfilled. It should help the believer to discern a reality which is not visible in the world and to live in its spirit. This is the "achievement" of the Christian, in the words of the apostle, "the victory which overcometh the world" (1 John 5:4).

Providence does not present a fixed pattern which was in itself always there but was first made known through Christ; it is continually being constructed by God. It consists in the first place in the guidance of the world which brings together natural processes with history—the history of humanity as a whole and of individual men. From the beginning God "foresees" all and fits it into the pattern of things in accordance with His wisdom. Through His operative power that streams from eternity into time He directs the course of events towards man's salvation. This is the first and preparatory stage. But Providence receives its proper form and significance through Christ.[35] Towards Christ and then from Christ streams a new history, and Providence is God's manner of guiding it. It is

35. For its nature, cf. Guardini, *Welt und Person*, pp. 137ff.

directed towards the realization of His kingdom and the creation of the new, holy world. God appeals for man's co-operation in this activity and promises him therein a new orientation of his life.

In the Sermon on the Mount we discover these words: "Seek ye first the kingdom of God and His justice, and all these things shall be added unto you" (Matt. 6:33). Providence, as heralded by Jesus, is to develop from this harmony of the believer with God's active and creative will. The pattern to which we pointed in dealing with destiny recurs on a new plane and with a new character; or, stated more precisely, the tension shown in destiny between existence as a whole and the individual is seen as a caricature of the relation made possible by the God of Providence between Himself and the believer. Life within it is no mere comfortable contentment; it involves the will towards a community of care and concern with God, an activity and a suffering in union with His will that makes the deepest possible demands. It is, in a very true sense, the "achievement" of faith and, because things continue seemingly to contradict it, "the victory which overcometh the world." When in faith and love a man shares God's care and concern for His kingdom, his existence receives a new direction and formation which descends upon him from the Father. This will be concealed by the old condition of the world and continuously disturbed by the as-yet unredeemed will of man, even that of the believer himself. Only at the end of time will it finally prevail and show forth its achievement, the new creation. In other words, Providence has ultimately an eschatological character.

In this whole context there can, however, be regress as well as progress in the sense that the note of destiny can revive in this relation to Providence and gain the upper hand. The possibility of seeing our relation to existence as destiny remains always latent like the other possibility of lapsing from faith and love. These changes are hard to analyse in detail. It may well be that ideas and feelings grow more rationalistic, more purely natural or mythological. Should the process continue, one's outlook can become so confused that events in one's life and in the world are again interpreted in terms of destiny. The world of Shakespeare in which ancient forms of man's experience, adapted to the taste of his day, seem to re-emerge, may perhaps be a classic example. The same tendency can be observed in modern philosophy of history, sociology and psychology. No doubt the mystical background has disappeared, and modern man could not have re-created it, and it is replaced by ideas of absolute determinism in historical, social, and individual behaviour. But this system of exact correspondences is in reality just another form of necessary destiny, in which existence is once again imprisoned and made meaningless.

The sense of destiny may re-emerge even in the thought of believers under the cover of revealed truth, as for instance in certain exaggerated views of the sovereignty of grace or of predestination. A God who destines the individual man to salvation or damnation without bringing his human freedom into the decision is no longer the God of the revelation of Jesus Christ but a revival of the ancient power of destiny concealed in Christian terminology.

Destiny and Judgment

Providence is the pattern of that activity by which God develops His kingdom. Within this pattern man's earthly welfare—his "eating, drinking, and being clothed" of the Sermon on the Mount—finds its true place. But everywhere the kingdom of God encounters opposition and Jesus' account of the last things warns us that this will not alter in the course of history, indeed that the opposition will grow more violent and fundamental (Matt. 24:1–31). God's kingdom is the absolute significance of history: this has to be defended against the claims not only of folly and evil but also of more serious, if less basic, natural objections.[36] It is despised, confused, ridiculed, and the possibility of this must always remain since it is of the essence of history that man should have a free hand in it. If the full significance of Providence is to be made clear, the process must come from God: this occurs in judgment.

But even human action remains, in the last resort, concealed. The attempts to interpret history are no more than approximations. All we can conclude from an individual's conduct and character is a moral probability, just sufficient as a foundation of social life, and there are times when those normally close to us create such an impression of being strangers that we ask ourselves whether we know them at all. With regard to ourselves, this sense of distance is replaced by an often more deceptive sense of familiarity, and the problems which arise from motives that criss-cross and operate at different levels become so complicated by the unconscious, and at times the conscious, refusal to see oneself as one is, and also by the force of pressure and instability, the self-deception of pride and vanity, passion and sloth, that the sincere man finds himself exclaiming with St. Paul: "Neither do I judge myself" (1 Cor. 4:3–4).

If the significant pattern of Providence is to be known, then it must be revealed ultimately in some special event, and this is the final judgment (Matt. 25:31–46; Rom. 14:10–12; Apoc. 20:11–13, and elsewhere). This doctrine is inextricably connected with that of Providence.

The Christian teaching on judgment states that after his time on earth man appears before God, who subjects him to His omniscient and just judgment and determines his eternal existence on the basis of his

36. Scandal properly consists in a confusion about sacred truth, an irritation against and refusal to accept the revelation of the living God: not through direct opposition, the root of which would be clearly evil, but on grounds that are real if less fundamental, and which seem to argue against that revelation and therefore invalidate its bases. Cf. Guardini, *The Lord*, pp. 43ff.

earthly life. Judgment is completed in two closely related acts. The first
190 follows after the death of each individual and has reference to his individual life; witness the parable of the rich spendthrift and the poor man, Lazarus (Luke 16:19–31). The verdict is that of eternal salvation, if the man has believed in and obeyed God, that of eternal loss if the man has repudiated God either totally or in some important decision that was not retracted. If his disposition was in general a good one but his life was still attached to evil in individual actions or at certain levels of his being, a period of purification awaits him, in which to cleanse and perfect himself.[37] The other act of judgment takes place at the end of time or, more exactly, after the second coming of Christ when time is at an end. Its judgment relates to humanity and its history; but also to the individual, in so far as he is included in the whole, and this is built up of individual lives. After this judgment there is no further purification, since that presupposes time; there is only eternity (Matt. 25:31–46).

In judgment all human action receives its final assessment: not merely in the sense that man moves from his provisional condition on earth to be seen perfectly from the absolute norms of truth and goodness but actually through a personal act of the living God. Judgment is the final expression of the historical character of experience. Existence had a genuine beginning in creation, which is a free act of God's majesty; it will have a genuine end given by the same God.[38] After this end there follows the assessment of existence for eternity.

---

37. On this whole question, cf. Guardini, *The Last Things* (New York, 1954), pp. 33ff., for the doctrine of purification after death. [New edition: *The Last Things* (Providence: Cluny, 2019).]

38. On this point the notion of judgment is in the sharpest possible contradiction to the modern interpretation of the world. This conceives it as "Nature," as what is simply given and established in its own right. It has neither beginning nor end and is regarded under the false notion of infinite progress or of an equally endless process of emergence and decline. Cf. Guardini, *Welt und Person*, pp. 1ff.

Judgment, whether individual or universal, takes away the disguise that man's temporal condition draws across his existence. Nature is the first to practise this concealment, attracting the human person into the pattern of organic life and physical laws and suggesting that he is a natural being like a crystal, plant, or animal. In its resistance to God, man's will uses this assimilation to steep itself in instincts, in intoxication and the fascination of the universe, and to throw off personal responsibility. Man's historical setting also is a form of concealment. In history, individual life remains to a large extent hidden. This it does primarily as *inwardness*, which can refuse to express itself or can express itself falsely. It remains hidden also because its motivations are tangled and operate at various levels, its causative factors cannot be unravelled, and because the past is over and the future not yet here. All historical action proceeds from one's detached interior life in the direction of the interior life of other persons; it proceeds from the present, conditioned by a vanished past, into a future that is unknown. The human will resisting God makes a cunning use of this concealment to escape responsibility through techniques of retreat and flight, of self-concealment and self-deception, of oblivion and the refusal to face realities. An even more profound concealment operates on the part of God. History presupposes freedom but freedom is the possibility of choice, ultimately for or against God. How that can happen when God sustains and fills everything, giving nature to being and order to spirit, is the mystery of history. It can occur in any case only because God is concealed in some way from man's temporal existence.[39] If God openly exercised His sovereignty, then His truth

39. "In some way"—this qualification states that God was "concealed" even before man sinned and when God had accorded him the privilege of immediate conversation with Him, as described in Genesis 2:15–25 and 3:8. Without "concealment" no decision between obedience and disobedience would be possible. But it had a character different from the "concealment" brought about by sin.

would illuminate everything, His holiness dominate everything, and the finite spirit could neither err nor choose evil. Consequently, God must in some way restrain Himself, limit Himself so as to allow the creature room for choice—an attitude that can only be understood as a kenosis. It is a beginning that reaches its last fulfilment in the kenosis of the Son of God, who becomes man and enters into history.[40] Temporal existence is in exceptional circumstances. God conceals Himself and appears to leave the temporal order to itself. He seems powerless, even unreal, because He maintains silence to leave free rein to the immanent patterns of the world. Truth and goodness appear divorced from power so that truth and goodness are seen as powerless and the employment of power is untrue and evil. The test of history lies in loyalty to truth and goodness even when this may appear foolishness in the actual state of affairs. This fundamentally is piety, to keep faith with God, who is seemingly impotent under the pressure of the objects and energies of immediate existence. It is threatened by scandal, the danger of wrong ideas about God on account of the power of untruth and the success of evil. The cunning human will in its resistance to God makes use of this last concealment in the temporal order to fabricate the lie of autonomy, to act as though God did not exist and as if history were the only reality and the fulness of reality, self-contained and self-sufficient.

Judgment takes away this concealment. God remains no longer shrouded in Himself. His truth illuminates spirit. His holiness permeates conscience. He assumes His full and open sovereignty. Truth and

40. We recall again the passage from Philippians that is so fundamental for Christology: "Let that mind be in you, which was also in Christ Jesus, who being in the form of God, thought it not robbery to be equal with God (though man, attached to evil, holds on to this anxiously) but (loving) emptied Himself, taking the form of a servant, being made in the likeness of men and in habit found as a man. He humbled Himself, becoming obedient unto death, even to the death of the cross" (2:5–8).

goodness are identified with power and reality. A being has the same share of reality as it has of truth, the same degree of life and beauty as it has of goodness. Evil is revealed as the great deceit. It seemed to confer "life"; it is now clear that it brings death, the "second death" from which there is no salvation (Apoc. 20:6,14). It appeared to possess power; it is now evident that it cannot create but can only destroy. It seemed to have meaning, to be necessary; it is now evident—and in this consists the eternal "scandal" (Rom. 9:33; 10:11; Phil. 1:20 and elsewhere)—that it is wholly superfluous. It seemed to be real but it is now patent, as is stated in the terrible passage from the Apocalypse, that it has no place at all in existence. From the judge "the earth and heaven flew away"—in so far as they were in evil—"and there was no place found for them" (20:11). This is the judgment: the true and holy God assumes His open sovereignty and calls man to his account.

In the particular judgment the association on which man's being rests—the personal I-Thou association to which God has elevated him—reaches its supreme point. Into the judgment that God passes on the individual no other person enters; there are only God and the man himself. We are reminded of the promise in the Apocalypse, according to which he who overcomes will receive "a new name written, which no man knoweth, but he that receiveth it" (2:17). In this absolute immediacy without barriers or veils God gives His final definition to the man. On the ground of his finite existence He establishes him in his eternal Being, expressed in the "new name." And now, from the loving harmony with God, from the fulness of the Divine mystery as it turns towards him, brighter than any concept, the man understands himself finally and completely. The rejected, of course, since he hates God, becomes not only a stranger to but also an enemy of God, and because God has established him too in Being, he becomes at once stranger and enemy to himself.

The same occurs at the universal judgment for history and for individuals that are part of it. If the particular judgment is in absolute privacy, in the I-Thou existential association of man with God, the universal judgment is a public one. It will show history to itself. It will reveal to humanity as a whole its own condition, how each individual is in it, and itself in every individual. The same applies to man's achievement. This also is subject to judgment. The Divine mystery that unfolds itself in Providence is the only medium through which this can be understood: the mystery from which all Being originates, and which remains impenetrable in temporal existence, will be understood in the larger mystery of God, now clearly manifested, the "All in all."

Judgment has a twofold significance. It means, to begin with, that God assumes His rights. After leaving free decision to man and making history possible through the limits He has imposed upon Himself, He calls man to account. This makes it clear that man's being, and through man the whole of created being, is determined by personal freedom. The way a man goes and the character he fashions for himself depend ultimately on his relation to God, that of obedience or disobedience. Judgment reveals the attitude man has adopted and that has affected the course of events, both in detail and as a whole. Behind the veil of time this course of events has made God seem unjust, unwise, and powerless; when the truth is unveiled He comes into His own.

Judgment also signifies that God gives man his right—the right which He established in creating man as a person. We have already spoken of the respect God pays to men, which distinguishes Providence fundamentally from destiny. Destiny is not in a position to respect man since it is a mere thing, but God is the absolute person, the "He" pure and simple, as He defined Himself in the words "I am Who am" (Exod. 3:14). Once He has created man as a person, He never forgets man's worth. He respects it "for His name's sake," because He respects His own dignity, of which human dignity is an image. Judgment reveals God's regard for man. Eternal life comes from temporal life—not as one phase of a biological process out of the preceding phase, or a psychological act from the impulses behind it, but as the final existential form of the particular man out of his personal decisions. This is made clear and firmly fixed in judgment. The essential foundation of judgment, justice, is that man is regarded not as a natural being but as a person, and his acts—in so far as they really are his acts—as personal and responsible behaviour.[41] As a person, man has a right to be taken seriously, as happens in judgment, reward, and punishment; and this right, which, be it repeated, is established by God, God secures to men in judgment. Judgment gives man also his rights against existence, in that it determines the "injustice" suffered by the individual on account of his body-soul heritage, corrupted through sin, the distribution of property and power, the mutual dependence of men upon one another, and the course of history.[42] It

41. The thought of God's absolute sovereignty should not be allowed to obscure the note of justice in judgment, nor should this be considered merely as the final act, decisive for eternity, of sovereign grace. The mystery of election hovers over the whole of man's existence, and both beginning and fulfilment are possible only because of grace. But it is just as certain that the judgment is not only the final determination and publication of the design of grace but a "judgment" also in the strict sense of a man's actions, words, and intentions. This is shown in the relevant passages from the New Testament. The formula of judgment runs as follows: "Come, ye blessed...for I was hungry and you gave me to eat... Depart from me, you cursed...for I was hungry and you gave me not to eat" (Matt. 25:24–35; 41–42). To give food to the hungry, in the sense in which Christ intends it, and to Christ *in* the hungry is possible only through faith and love, that is, through grace; it is at the same time a genuine individual human act, proceeding freely from man and therefore capable of being realized or refused.

42. We cannot attribute this injustice to any particular person. However much individual men co-operate with it, its burden is the confusion of existence at its very roots. This confusion, it is true, is a consequence of the sin of the first man, which was the beginning and source of all subsequent sins, and also of this problem we have been studying. To that extent, it is justice but justice considered generally; this does not do away with the fact that injustice is done to the individual. For the individual is not only a member of the whole race but also, as a person, he is an individual. If his life and work are adversely affected by history and society, injustice exists and remains.

gives him, finally, his right against other men in making clear, condemning, and punishing the injustice they have committed against him.

Conviction and punishment, however, only create justice, they do not compensate for injury, and we must therefore suppose that God's immense and generous riches will make good what has not been made good by any created agency.[43]

God unveils His Providence in judgment. He takes up the basic questions about the meaning of existence which men have been continually asking throughout history: "Why did that happen to me?" "Why am I what I am?" "Why do I exist at all?" Destiny is eternally silent. The God of Providence answers in judgment. His holiness and justice both accept and demand the complete clarification of history; this will constitute the final revelation of God's mind. It is His "Justification."[44]

Judgment will make clear to every man the network of necessity on which his life has been based, both in general and in detail, and also the sources and meaning of the events which have determined his life, his motives in their complexity and at their various levels, his dispositions, in stability, decline, and collapse. In addition, the freedom of his decisions, his free activity as such, has to be shown to him in a light which only that God can provide who established the creature in Being. He will now realize for the first time what existed and what occurred, and how his existence has been fashioned from all this. This applies to those others with whom he was associated, not only individuals but also

43. This is suggested by the words of Jesus: Matt. 29:29; Mark 10:29–30; Luke 18:28–30.

44. The idea that God requires to be justified in view of the questions raised by men is an essential part of Biblical revelation. God's action is directed to persons, not things; the question of origin and meaning is therefore not enough. One has to inquire into justice even against God, and God allows this prerogative to men. This theme is continually present in the Psalms. It is the theme also of the Book of Job and the answer given there, though not yet complete, at least points the way to a solution. The full answer will be given in judgment.

community, from family to humanity at large.[45] But it applies in a very special manner to himself. Now at last will he understand himself, know what he was, what he has done, and how he has built up his existence from his own initial freedom. At last he can and must take over the world with himself in it and thus fully realize his existence. Finally, he will understand what seemed to be chance in his temporal life, for he will see his individual existence at last in the pattern of the whole and, on the other hand, the general pattern from his individual existence. This final balance of relations leaves no room for the feeling of chance and its more marked expression in senselessness, malice, and error: all the less so since in judgment, whether this be in love and adoration or under the force of God's omnipresent power, man recognizes his own contingency of Being. Only now does a man acquire that understanding regard for his own Being, of which we have been speaking, which is both clarity and courage, insight and obedience, truth as well as love.[46] God's Providence is justified throughout.

This is done mainly through a full manifestation of God's mind. In a general way it was already realized in revelation, which declared that God acted and continues to act from love. It did so in a message that surpassed man's natural understanding and had to be grasped by faith. The degree to which man grows in harmony with God is the measure also in which he grows in understanding of God's mind. Yet veils still remain: all the time there sounds the lamentation, "Lord, why?" Complete clarity for individual and universe comes only with judgment. Then at last man

45. Consequently, the judgment must not be private only, it has also to be public. In fact, it is the public event *par excellence*; maybe we should derive the essential character of all genuine publication—as distinct from communication—from judgment at the end of time.

46. This supposes that the rejected whose fundamental attitude is hatred, not love, does not understand himself. We are not thinking of a question which fails to receive an answer but of a final imprisonment within untruth, conditioned by evil.

will be allowed to know why God acted thus here and now, and how
198 this "thus," this "here" and "now" find their place in the grand pattern of times and places, how the singular event has sustained the totality of history and how the course of this totality has been made concrete in the singular event. In the measure that God chooses, and is suitable for man, the abyss of God's freedom, what Scripture terms His "Design" will open and it will be evident how far everything was love—even to the original *act-fact* of all, which provided possibility and place for all individual facts, simply that God created the world and why and for what purpose.

Judgment will also reveal the ways of God's grace: His redemption and forgiveness, His operations and His paths, His enlightenment and assistance, vocation and guidance, foundations and constructions. The mystery will be unveiled that grace is responsible for all operations—beginning, continuance, and fulfilment—and yet that man is responsible for all his action: a mystery expressed earlier in the sentence that the more forcibly God's grace is operating, so much the more personally free is man.

Judgment in point of fact is the completion of the realm of grace. Christ is the fulness of grace. No sooner does He approach a man than He sets before him the choice of hearing or not hearing Him and this is decisive for the man's life. John's Gospel tells us that "this is the judgment, because the light is come into the world, and men loved darkness rather than the light" (John 3:19). And this judgment forces its way on to the plane of reality and becomes history. Christ's rejection by the chosen people found expression in the destruction of Jerusalem. From this standpoint, the judgment at the end of time is at once the final revelation and the fulfilment of God's dispensation of grace that has been operating through time and history.

Judgment reposes on the second coming of the Incarnate Son, who brought to earth that Redemption which one man accepts while another rejects it. It is thus the final act in the series of Divine actions, the conclusion of the entire history of His creation, Redemption, and sanctification. Its significance is found in this, that it not only reveals what *is* but it passes explicit "judgment" on it and provides its final definition.

But why, it may be asked, is this necessary? Why is it not sufficient if temporal life is illuminated and fulfilled interiorly in the light of eternal clarity?

In the first place, the particular character of the "process of salvation" is continued in judgment. This is neither purely natural nor metaphysical but historical and it proceeds by decisions taken and acts performed. In consequence, it must be brought to an end by an act that is eminently historical. But perhaps something further may be said about the significance of this process of judgment.

Logic teaches that the conclusive act of knowledge is the judgment; it is a proposition which places the object under concepts already known so as to define it without ambiguity, for instance, "Two is the half of four." But this does not exhaust the meaning of judgment. When I have answered every possible query about the object, have gained every conceivable insight into it, and can demonstrate that this *is* the situation, then no doubt remains, in the sense that I could have no reason for thinking it could be otherwise. Two is always the half of four, never a third or any other ratio. But does this knowledge satisfy me completely? No, because there does remain a kind of non-fulfilment, a lack of absolute finality. This is not due to confusion in the questioner's mind which prevented him from having real knowledge; it raises a problem which affects the very nature of knowledge. It is true that not all men feel this problem. Positive and rationalist individuals, for example, are so impressed by definition and insight that they are completely satisfied with them. But there are other persons—their number and quality are not negligible—who apply to what is called "knowledge" a standard that is not wholly satisfied

by the objects it can attain. Their desire for knowledge outsoars their
200 capacity for knowledge. "Knowledge" is the realization of a significant content by a concrete knowing act. The content is valid, that is, absolute. The knowing act, on the other hand, is finite and contingent. Man's mind rises above his own finitude towards the Absolute, but in himself, in his being, he is not absolute. He approximates to the Absolute but never attains to it. Perfect knowledge would imply that the concrete knowing act would correspond to the content known, and would be as absolute in the order of being as the content is in the realm of values. But this is possible only in the case of God, not in that of a finite spirit. The latter knows well that the validity of what is known is absolute but he cannot achieve this himself in any corresponding act. The result is an inadequacy which all the power of insight cannot overcome. An extra-noetic act is necessary in which the knower as living person enters into the relation between *subject* and *object* of knowledge, and "decides" that "two is the half of four." It pledges its honour that this is so and thus puts an end to that lack of finality we have mentioned. This takes place in judgment.[47] What has been said about the effective relation of the knowing act to truth also applies to the relation of man's whole existence to its significance. Eternal life denotes the final establishment of individual existence in salvation, that is, in God. To this man cannot attain by his own powers: partly because salvation is grace and is therefore beyond man's natural grasp

47. With the kind of person described, the decisive character of judgment is always noticed. The inadequacy is not removed altogether but softened, and it still provides a source from which a fundamental doubt could rise as to the possibility of knowledge, namely, Scepticism. Scepticism consists not in uncertainty in the determination of facts or in the obscurity of logical processes but in a feeling that knowledge as such cannot reach its objective. Hence the cravings, peculiar to such natures, for an immediate certainty in intuition and, in the last resort, in mystical experience. The Platonic theory of an intuition of the Ideal Form seems to have this as one of its psychological roots, and Augustine's doctrine of an illumination through intelligible light can be understood only with this presupposition.

but also—and this concerns us here—because it is not only absolute but God, the Absolute Himself, whereas man is finite. Consequently, a "definition," a "judgment" is necessary. Man does not have the capacity to draw this out of himself for this is no partial act, the final indefiniteness of which could be determined through his personal action; it is a question of man's existence as such. Only God can make such a definition and he does formulate it in judgment. This judgment fixes a man's relation to eternal life, that is to say, his relation to God Himself, from the history which he has experienced and in which he has played his part. It rests, as has been said, on man's actions and therefore it is made by justice: it is an expression of God's sovereignty which no limits can confine, and it thus fulfils the order of grace. The man must accept it from God's freedom. Once accepted, he understands and confesses that it is right.

Through the verdict of salvation or rejection judgment both manifests and completes Providence. What still remains incapable of being understood, since this understanding would presuppose a Divine insight, this remnant of mystery becomes a source and content of adoration.

But even this is an incorrect manner of speaking. For it is no "remnant" left over for want of the power to grasp it fully. What is left is something essential—the quality that belongs to the entire pattern of things, even to understanding itself, since the All-glorious and Ineffable God who created and directed it is also its judge. The man who abides in love will experience this quality as glory and adore it with joyfulness.

Providence and the Values of Destiny

What, then, is the attitude of life, as conceived under Providence, to those values that are realized in the philosophy of destiny? We shall conclude this chapter also with a number of thoughts and suggestions.

A strong man would surely protest against a belief in Providence that treats him as a child. Will not the feeling that he is an object of loving care get on his nerves, with the result that the idea of a conflict with destiny, despite its grimness, will seem a nobler conception than this world of love he is being offered? In this life sheltered by Providence what place is left for man's impulses towards wide-ranging plans and adroit adaptation, towards swift initiative and defensive action, to discovery and adjustment, to the tenacious enforcement of his own will as also to the restraint that helps a man develop? Where is the maturity of a man stirred to a sense of his proper task and responsibility? Where is the element of tragedy which may make existence hard but crowns it with glory? The answer to this objection is complicated by many a factor in exterior Christian practice that appears to provide some justification.

Let us first, however, put the question in its just proportions. The comparison should not be drawn between a weak Christian and an heroic believer in destiny. Certainly, there is a type of man who lets a good-natured heavenly Father look after him and himself becomes weak and lazy. But there are also negative phenomena on the side of the believer in destiny: the feeling that one is abandoned to an irresponsible force, the sense of a degrading meaninglessness, a stolid resignation to the unintelligible and the overpowering, that dark dread of the very foundation of life, and none of these produces noble results. And then, a position within Providence, as we have insisted, is not only a gift and help but a task and demand as well. What is essential to belief in Providence is not that we should throw ourselves into the arms of a friendly Father who puts all things into order but that we should participate in God's care for His kingdom, and share the responsibility for this absolutely decisive concern. Fundamental to the gospel of Providence is an appeal for the highest personal earnestness, and this relation to Providence is realized in the measure in which this responsibility is accepted and put into practical effect.

The way in which it is realized in the concrete depends on the various conditions found in the character of a period or a people, in temperament and environment and the special circumstances of an individual life. Within this general framework the values we have been examining reappear, purified and raised to a higher level. The figures of great Christian personalities, in particular the saints, present us with a formal phenomenology of the ways in which firm and rich human values may be realized in relation to Providence. The serene and absolute confidence achieved by a Francis of Assisi in unconditional surrender to God's will is impressively distinct from the prudence of an Ambrose of Milan, rooted in a long administrative tradition. The lives of great ambassadors of the faith contain all the combative bravery and the heroism of lonely deaths, assumed into an awareness of an eternal life, established in God. The essence of the Stoic attitude was found in the shedding of layers and levels of existence till the innermost core was reached; but this cannot be more perfectly realized than by the great ascetics in the radical pursuance of the principle, "the one thing necessary." As for the love that touches the heart, stirs it from one sacrifice to another, breaks through obstacle after obstacle, and is wholly consumed in one single flame, the destinies of heroic lovers most assuredly do not go beyond the experiences of an Elizabeth of Hungary or a Frances de Chantal. Much more could be said, especially to note that those values and attitudes prominent in the lives of outstanding men also make themselves manifest in other lives according to capacity and resolution. The relation to Providence is their final truth and it is accordingly all-embracing. It can be realized in as many different ways as there are different categories and degrees of men.

But this supposes, as has been observed, that a Christian must take his responsibility with real earnestness, and a candid examination of the facts forces us to admit that emphasis on authority, however necessary, and on the obedience due to it, has diverted men's attention from the responsibility of individual judgment, moral decision, and personal participation to an extent that might well disturb us. In this respect, there is a good deal that calls for reflection and amendment.

One reason for this tendency has been a certain trend of thought deriving from human progress. Man's power over Nature and also over his own human nature has already advanced over a wide range and, as far as Nature is concerned, no one can foresee its limits. Nietzsche has provided us with a new assessment of power which makes it a kind of religion. It is seen as the one all-embracing factor, transcending truth, justice, and humanity, and claiming an absolute sovereignty. From this there arises the question, which men have long since forgotten to ask, namely: What is the significance of power? Clearly, it is ambiguous. It was one of the errors of a primitive belief in progress to imagine that because man gains greater mastery over Nature and can exercise wider technical control, he can take his own value for granted. In reality, power is determined by the value which it serves. In consequence, the growth of power brings with it a continually growing danger. When we consider the energies at man's command, it is no mere academic question to inquire whether they do not create a danger not only for his physical status but even for the balance of his psychological and spiritual life.

Power is good to the extent to which it is wielded responsibly and morally, and secured by sound judgment and self-control. Its first presupposition is that a man fits himself into the pattern by which God directs the world. In contrast, a Christian readily forgets that he is responsible for the world, *positively* responsible: he must take care that nothing wrong occurs in his sphere of life and also that the things of the world are in proper order. He must therefore realize that our modern scientific and technical development has raised problems which did not exist previously. And if immense disasters are to be avoided, these have to be solved—in the first place through the development of a moral and spiritual outlook sufficiently mature to deal with the massive forces now at man's disposition.

The idea has been aired in non-Christian circles—we have commented on this in an earlier passage—that man, now fully adult, must take over the rights and responsibilities, the positions and achievements, formerly attributed to God. In other words, in this context, that Providence must be handed over to man, who has now advanced so far that he can assume ultimate control. If the believer objects that he would require omnipotence for this, he is informed that "omnipotence" was the primitive and absolute term which man, not yet adult, applied to the great "Other" to describe a position which he could not yet assume. This was quite right as long as he needed this relief to develop unhindered but he no longer requires such forbearance. He can now do it and therefore should do it; if any man cannot, then let him make way for a stronger man to carry on. Man is not, however, to be omnipotent in the sense in which an outdated metaphysics applied that expression to God; he must know what are the real possibilities latent in the world and himself, take them in hand, and set to work. The true human omnipotence is to be discovered in this self-reliant advance into the unknown. Should the believer again object that the sovereign direction of the world calls for omniscience, he is told that this is no ready-made omniscience corresponding to an absolute but non-existent Being but that of man in the world, whose knowledge may indeed be finite but is continually developing. When man boldly stakes his faculty of knowledge and begins an inquiry, resolved to shrink from no consequences, then the pathway into the unknown opens before him, and this is genuine omniscience. If he has resolved to accept all consequences, he can take Providence into his own hands, for this should be conceived not after the pattern of an absolute Being but as brought down into the region of the finite and the human. The real "absolute" consists in man's determination to make this transition, in which, greatly daring, he "decides" what is and what is not.

Consequently, Providence, in this new meaning, denotes the ability
206 to foresee the future, to see through the network of causes and distinguish what results from them; or, more precisely, to penetrate as far as is necessary to detect the most urgent elements, what corresponds, for instance, to the historical situation. It denotes a sensitiveness to the inner rhythm of history, the creative ground of the world process. Being is rich with possibility; it provides what is demanded from it by a will strong enough to make the demand. It is plastic throughout and it conforms itself to the will able to command it. Beneath all forms and forces lies the womb of becoming. Man must not wait for what proceeds from it; he must determine what is to come. Man, now grown to man's estate, must learn to plan and cultivate, and to call into being what has not yet existed. He must learn to judge when it is time for something to come into existence and also when some other thing has had its day and should disappear to make way for something else.

Man has only himself to direct his concerns. He actually directed his life even in the past. But, because he was not then adult, he did so unconsciously or, rather, his nature did this in him, and that this might happen securely, he invented the protective formula that it was the work of God. But he must now understand that he is director and must take this direction resolutely in hand. He must come to know himself, both his conscious and his unconscious self. He will then recognize the signs of his own creative inwardness, dreams and illnesses, premonitions and warnings. He will understand the real significance of myths and dogmas, and whereas till now, in his efforts to make progress, he had to set them aside for the sake of freedom, once he is sure of himself he will understand that they express one thing only, namely, himself and his mastery of the world, and so he can take them into his service. Education at last receives its full import: it is no longer an attempt of the grown-up to fit the lives of growing youth into pre-existing patterns; it is work for the future in an absolute sense. It does not take man as he is but it sketches the pattern of what he should be and, knowing the laws of Nature's operations, it realizes this consciously from one generation to another.

At the same time, science approximates more and more nearly to the structural form of Nature and makes it possible for technology to work on its basic elements. For the educated man it provides a field of even richer possibilities just as education also produces the man to make full use of them. These are the ideas present, more or less explicitly, in the minds of today. It is easy to detect the insolence and danger in them but much harder to see their good points; but they do contain good points. The world has been entrusted to man's care in a far different way than was envisaged in the past: not only the external world, the world of objects, forms, and forces, but also the interior world, the living, essential man with body and soul. Man's power over the world is growing fantastically great. God's design to create man after His own image (Gen. 1:26), that is, with the capacity for dominion, clearly and even disturbingly transcends the ideas that obtained in ages more restricted in outlook and at the same time more secure. The believer has tended to underestimate the dominion God has entrusted to him and has taken too placid a view of the measure, even of the nature, of his responsibility. He has represented all this in the form of a good-hearted father, creating a workshop for his son and providing materials and tools for him to do a good job, while the man himself is careful to see that everything is kept in its proper order. This son can no doubt destroy a tool or waste material or occasion all sorts of trouble but not beyond certain limits, since the pattern of his own Being is withdrawn from his control. The picture belongs to that stage of history, to which the somewhat vague term "organic" is applied, when man's power of initiative did not go beyond certain limits, dictated by immediate natural forms. But it is no longer applicable and there is little sense in reiterating that the present situation is dangerous. Of course it is dangerous. But we have no ground for thinking that all danger has been

excluded from the real association with the world that God has imposed on us. From the fact that God created a free creature and placed the world under his control we have to draw more far-reaching conclusions than used to be drawn, as regards both the seriousness of God's demands and the danger in the power entrusted to man. We must not regard God's control of the world as a system of protection in which men live piously and securely; if we do, we are leaving the grandeur of human existence to the unbeliever, and belief becomes identified with timidity. All grandeur belongs of course to God. What inspires fear or awe is a sign of the God whose first words, as He encounters man, are "Fear not." The courage to give shape to the world through science and technology is a part of His control of the world, and the Christian must be ready to do this.

Man's claim to take over Providence is both insolent and fraught with disaster since it does violence to the royal dominion of God, to whom alone belongs dominion. Yet it remains true that God's Providence has made use of human foresight, direction, and formative skill in its designs to a far greater extent than has hitherto been understood. Consequently, Christian belief must develop an ethic of self-dependence, an awareness of the duties and rights of man, entrusted with the world's development, and a corresponding power of action.[48]

---

48. This is not a doctrine of Activism. Man has his duty and work to fulfil, wherever he happens to be. Should temperament and religious vocation draw him to an interior life, he will follow it. If he belongs to that large number of people whose means and resources have been taken away in the disasters of recent years, so that all they can do is to gain a livelihood and, for the rest, trust in Divine Providence, then this is what they do; they ought to realize that, if they do this properly, they will be making their contribution to the solution of world problems—perhaps more so than others whose names are household words. In the long run, the judgment will reveal who have been the real workers. We are concerned here with one aspect of the Christian relation to the world. This must be understood if the significance of the historical moment or, in more Christian terms, the will of God is not to be neglected.

Excursus: The Element of Tragedy

One further question may be chosen from the many which arise from belief in Providence, namely, whether the note of tragedy is to be found in the pattern of Being which Providence directs. This can appear in the most varied circumstances. Poetry, and especially tragedy, intensifies and interprets it till its nature is made fully clear. A rapid survey will distinguish some of its forms and bring out more obviously its genuine character.

Our first Western experience of it is found in ancient tragedy. This rests on the presupposition that every sphere in the world has its inner meaning and is divine. Man lives in different spheres and they thus have power over him and rights against him—all of them, in fact, even when they contradict one another. When Paris steals Helen, he is obeying the command of Aphrodite and she is friendly; at the same time he is violating Menelaus's marriage, and Hera, protectress of the marriage bond, is hostile. This does not imply that the realm of Eros is bad and that of the family is good. Properly speaking, both are good—that is, essential for existence and powerful—and both make their claims on man. Yet they contradict one another; an impasse is reached which leads to catastrophe. The man Paris and, because of his action, the whole of Troy are destroyed. Both deities fulfil their purpose; Being again surges upwards and the stream of life again flows freely. Such is the event at the beginning of a whole cycle of legends that gives birth to a series of tragedies. This is typical of early ancient tragedy, rooted in a mythical ground and belonging to existence as a whole.[49]

Shakespeare's tragedy is closely related to this. One might say that ancient tragedy reappears with him in the pattern of soul, spirit, and character. An individual man has a particular disposition, with instincts

49. I cannot treat further the ethical and psychological effects in this kind of tragedy.

and urges, immediate values and ideals. No sooner does he express himself than he comes into conflict with the "other" person also expressing his personality. Once again, we have the impasse that leads to collapse. The conflict may be set forth in ethical terms and then the collapse is a moral one; but basically, it is not this, as it was not this in ancient tragedy. Its real concern is with man's world, which is so constructed that the individual man, once he is strong and acts as his nature demands of him, clashes inevitably with some other man and with the world as a whole. Then comes catastrophe and after it the way is made clear again. There remains a heritage which life carries forward.[50]

These would appear to be the original forms of tragedy.

Modern classical tragedy, in its French and German form, converts this into an ethical problem. It portrays a great man with marked qualities and energies, both good and bad. Basically, he wants what is right but he fails at certain points. This failure is not so great that it corrupts the whole picture but it does strike a violent note and through this the absolute character in ethics is emphasized. The evil done by the great man, whose moral responsibilities are very great, appears in all its abomination and is very severely punished. The hero collapses. The moral order is strikingly vindicated through the sacrifice of an existence so rich in promise, and the man himself receives a new character. Over the disaster

---

50. These forms are emphasized by some outstanding modern authors, in whose eyes lofty values, in particular love and honour, are so exalted that they can find no proper room in the world as it exists (Balzac, Dostoyevsky, and Conrad among them). The same is true of the philosophy of mere finitude deriving from Nietzsche, which develops ideas and sentiments from the old Northern world. Its starting point is existence as known in experience. The insufficiency of such experience—it argues—is no reason for concluding that there must be an absolute principle; this insufficiency must be understood as the very essence of existence. All that we have is this existence, finite in every respect; there is nothing besides. It must therefore be accepted and its meaning discovered entirely within itself. This makes existence essentially tragic.

there hovers a soft radiance. It is difficult to say what exactly this signifies but fundamentally it is a kind of afterglow of a Christian eternity. At any rate, after the shock of guilt and disaster, it induces in the onlooker a mood of confidence, impossible of closer definition.

As one last form we may mention the tragedy in late nineteenth- and early twentieth-century drama. Its main theme is disaster. There are no longer any really binding values. Individuals and society are rich in values and energies but within themselves they carry the seeds of disintegration. Basically, they are neither capable of existing nor indeed worthy to exist, and the tragedy manifests how destruction is inevitable. Experience of this tragedy shows us what Ibsen calls the all-devouring lie in life. A man sees that no improvement is possible and he accepts disaster, either in hopeless resignation or in a mood of furious courage, knowing that only thus can a place be made for a better man.

Now, in what does this tragic element consist? These reflections suggest that it consists in the inevitability of destiny in a world completely self-enclosed so that man can make no appeal from it to another world. This self-enclosure no longer exists once revelation has been given because in Christ the world has become open. He is essentially the "Way" from the living God to us, and from ourselves to the living God. Through Christ we can appeal from the immediate course of events to the hidden significance of Divine Providence. Even the most terrible occurrence is under Providence; even the darkest disaster has its relation to the Resurrection.

Now, does not this mean that a basic note of grandeur vanishes from existence, a note that is terrifying and yet glorious? We find ourselves back with the same question. The answer is, once again, No. What vanishes is the note of inevitability and, judged by the touchstone of a person's inviolable rights, the meaninglessness of an existence conditioned by destiny. Perhaps certain values are lost, such as can thrive only on the ground of utter hopelessness; but this does not conceal the fact that such an attitude is a radical abandonment of all values. And since here we are dealing with ultimate matters, let a man remain wide awake and listen very intently; he will soon realize that this praise of tragic values is, generally speaking, so much chatter without substance.

The Christian approach rests upon an earnestness deeper and stronger than, and indeed altogether different in kind from, that of tragedy. Whether tragedy be concerned with life or honour or work or the future or, in short, with any courageous attitude, it rests on the pathos of infinity, of continuing process, of the "All" or, at the opposite pole, of tragic finitude. And both of these belong to the illusion of unredeemed consciousness. The Christian is disillusioned in the deepest sense but this disillusionment brings him not to what is matter of fact and banal but to the truth. As Christ disenchanted the "religious" element and replaced it with firm faith and obedience to the living God, so also tragedy, with its pathos and despair, has been disenchanted and replaced by a Christian earnestness with its courageous grasp of truth and its imperturbable hope. It is far easier to hurl oneself into a Dionysiac "all" or to take one's stand in an "exposed" finitude than to understand that for a good will every situation leads towards what is eternally good—through a truth that tolerates no exaltation, a justice that submits each action to infallible judgment, and a sacrifice for ever consecrated with the sentence: "Father, not my will but Thy will be done" (Matt. 26:39).

But the problem still requires to be studied at a deeper level. Does not the Divine and created reality manifested in revelation contain elements that must be considered tragic—and so clearly indeed that the whole concept of God and the existence determined by God are marked with the same tragic stamp? How can evil exist, and the destruction caused by evil exist, in a world God created? God wanted the world to be good and healthy; has it not in fact proved a failure? The answer is that God wished the world to reach its culmination in man's freedom and He must therefore give this freedom the power of decision, even against Himself. But, it is urged, God knew from eternity what form that decision would take. Why, then, did He create the world at all? One possible reply is that these questions touch upon the realm of absolute mystery and therefore both the questions and any answers we try to give them are necessarily inadequate. None the less, a man has to put these questions; it is the only way he can express the most disturbing note in all existence. Why, then, did God bring a creature into being when He foresaw the way it would go?

We may put the question even more precisely. God did not leave the world to its injustice and evil, while Himself remaining in Olympian serenity. He embraces it with an earnestness peculiar to Himself. This earnest concern is gradually shown in the course of revelation. We read that God fashioned the world after His ideas and man in His own likeness. This means not only that the world as an achievement is good but also that the Creator impressed on it the significant forms that are founded in His own Being (cf. John 1:1–3) and has thus, as it were, staked His own honour upon it. In the account of creation (Gen. 1) He repeatedly refers to it as "good," and ultimately as "very good," and He guarantees its worth. Then man misuses his freedom against the God who gave it to him. God does not, however, let the creature fall away; He begins the work of redemption. He approaches the creature, comes towards it, is present to it, acts on and together with it.[51] This

51. On the significance of these ideas, which might seem anthropomorphic but are really fundamental, see Guardini, *Die Offenbarung* (1940), pp. 53ff. To understand revelation, it is essential to transcend the natural-mythological and the philosophic-absolute categories and to think in personal and historical terms. This was done basically in the Old Testament and the same process is continued in the man who approaches it with faith and confidence. This is its special meaning for Christian existence. Once the Old Testament is depreciated, the attack is switched to the New Testament, which is then treated from the standpoints of philosophy and psychology and becomes meaningless. It is no accident that the most recent attacks upon the New Testament have started from the Old Testament.

process reaches its summit in the Incarnation. This signifies that God manifests Himself within the world, speaks to and acts in it, and also that He enters into a union with the creature closer than anything that can be conceived. When the Son assumes human nature into the unity of His Being, He elevates created Nature into the Divine life. To be sure, this human nature is absolute in its purity. The eternal Son comes, however, as Redeemer, with the consequence that the whole Being of Christ belongs to the category of "for us." Thus, He makes sin His own, not as an act He has committed but as a guilt He has representatively assumed.

But how can this happen? Does it not contradict all that is meant by God? Is He not the Absolute, perfect in Being and power, worth and significance, action and happiness? Must not His work have been inevitably perfect? How can the world He created go this way? How can He, after this has happened, have anything further to do with it? What kind of God is it that acts thus? Is He anything more than man's projection of himself into divinity? Man is accustomed to taking risks in his work, and meeting with failure, and none the less holding on to it out of loyalty, necessity, or sheer desperateness, trying to save what he can of it. Surely, such an idea of God must be rejected by any mature mind?

The challenge of revelation is here seen in its sharpest outlines. Once I assess it, for instance, by standards drawn from my feeling for the religious or my concept of absolute Being, then I start dissociating myself from these points we have been examining, and after passing through several degrees of rationalization and moralizing I end with a radical denial. If I wish to avoid this course, then I must take revelation with complete seriousness. I must not judge it from outside, with preconceptions derived from the world, whether empirical or rational, but I must place myself inside it and use it to assess the world, including my own experience and thinking. Then I can no longer say that God cannot do this or that because it would contradict the concept of pure divinity. I have to say that according to revelation God does this and reveals Himself in it to me. This is a Copernican inversion of thought, part of that "conversion" demanded by Christ, on which Christian existence is based. It includes the religious conversion of the heart to God, the ethical conversion from evil to good, and in addition the conversion from natural to Christian thinking. Christian thought does not proclaim that this and that are the principles of right action, and therefore revelation is to be accepted or rejected in so far as it conforms to or contradicts them, but rather that the beginning lies with revelation and that what it declares to be true is the truth.[52] Consequently, in spiritual conversion I have to acknowledge God as being, first and foremost in His Being, the absolute Lord, who reveals Himself in this sovereign glory and declares: This is myself.[53] From this standpoint, the doctrine of creation tells us that God's mind is such that, though He is in need of nothing and is indeed absolute Lord, He has willed a finite world at His side and before Himself—it is impossible to find any category in which to set this basic relation of our existence—and has willed this "from now on and for

52. The mind has good reasons for recognizing that this claim is justified and processes of natural reasoning converge towards it. Experience constantly assures us that the mind that accepts this and makes its way through the narrow gate attains on the further side to a height and clarity in which for the first time the reality of the world is unveiled. This would require a further analysis of its own. Here we are concerned only with the distinction.

53. This is expressed clearly and forcibly in the event which provides the foundation for all right thinking about God, namely, the vision narrated in Exodus 3:14 on Mount Horeb, when God answers Moses' inquiry as to His name with the words "I am who am." And He adds forthwith: "So shalt thou speak to the sons of Israel: He who is has sent me to you." With this, God repudiates every name and concept drawn from the world: but not absolutely, for He does speak of Himself in different Scriptural passages as the living, the holy, the just, the Almighty God, among other terms. But at this particular moment on Mount Horeb, at this decisive point of history, He is declaring: There is no name you can draw from the world for me, and you must accept me thus. Subsequently, you may find other names from experience and knowledge but only after a conversion in faith and obedience.

ever." His mind is such that He has willed the reality of creation to its culminating point in freedom, and this denotes that the creature can act with genuine initiative, according to, but even against, God's will; that He foresaw that the latter would happen and none the less willed freedom. God's mind is such that He did not repudiate the rebellious and ruined creature but held it fast, and even assumed it into His own life through the Incarnation of His Son so that "henceforth"—the word is a foolish one but any alternative would be still more inadequate—we have no longer a "God existing for Himself alone" but a God from whose triune life the second person, the Logos, became man.

Revelation tells us that this is the mind of God; and the message is so astounding that as a rule the believer does not comprehend it. But if he does, there is the danger that it will be basically rejected with the verdict that "there just cannot exist a God like that." Such a God contradicts the categories of the spirit, the perceptions of religious experience, in fact everything that man assumes as belonging properly to God. It is the danger of scandal. This is overcome through the act of conversion in faith, the burden of which is as follows: It is revelation that is speaking. God is what He shows us that He is. What man chooses from his own experience to call "God" is a side issue, a stepping-stone for faith; but if it becomes rigid and fossilized, then you have the illusion, which is latent in religion, by which Nature or some idealized picture is made Divine. But there is no such divinity, through the whole range from the numina of natural religions to the absolute Being of the philosophy of religion. The God who does "exist," the true, living God, is the God who manifests Himself in revelation. It is with this God that man has to do, whether he likes it or not, in time and in eternity.[54]

54. Besides, natural knowledge of God predisposes us to recognize that He transcends all earthly measures and therefore He alone can declare who He properly is.

What mind is this which expresses itself in God's creation of the finite so that what is unnecessary, what is of its nature superfluous, should be "at His side" and "before Him"? That He should allow freedom the room to operate against His own will, which after all He must will since He is supreme holiness? Or that He should bring the world into being, although He knows what way it will go? That after its fall He should pursue it, Himself become man and assume its guilt-laden being into His Being through the mystery of representative atonement? But this mind is Love. And we have at once to make a further distinction to preserve the purity of this sacred concept. It is not that affective, ethical, personal attitude to which we normally apply the term, merely purified from all limitation and able to express its full compass; it is God's mind as announced in revelation and as it is manifested to man when, sustained by grace, he accepts it with faith and fulfils it.

Once again, what is the answer to our question? Is not such an attitude on God's part a tragic one? Are we not literally compelled—and here the problem appears at its final, most sacred and decisive level—are we not literally compelled to speak of a "destiny" in God, and indeed of a tragic destiny? Have we not here a vision of destiny in the full and absolute sense, of which our earthly destiny is but a confused echo?

It would seem nonsense to talk of destiny in connection with God. He is the absolute Lord; there is nothing that can stand over against Him from which destiny could derive. He is also Lord of Himself; there is no necessary tendency to which He must conform Himself. God is absolutely free. But revelation tells us that He loves, truly and really loves.[55] If one man's relation to another is wholly disinterested, this contact makes no deep impression. There is a protective wall between them

55. On the problem of love and freedom in God, cf. Guardini, *Welt und Person*, pp. 130ff.; also *Die christliche Liebe*, pp. 19ff.

that excludes personal encounter. It is a case of him, not myself, and of myself, not him. As soon as he begins to love that other person, the wall disappears. He becomes, as it were, open: what affects the other now affects him. Love transforms the condition of the loved one into the destiny of the lover. Through love destiny enters into the personal sphere. This is precisely what has happened with God. Revelation informs us that His attitude towards the creature from the beginning was love, that this love continued even after man's revolt, that it seemed to grow even greater as it was forced outwards from a deeper source. We can scarcely avoid the statement that the creature has become a "destiny" for God. This is shown concretely in Christ, who is the epiphany of the invisible God. What leads us to the inner secret of God's mind is no theory of absolute values and motives but our vision of Christ's attitude and the development of Christ's life. Surely, His attitude and His experience have a note of most tragic destiny?

These thoughts seem to have involved us in a vicious circle. We endeavoured to show that we could not speak about destiny in reference to Christ, since whatever happens to Him happens in the most perfect harmony between Himself and the Father. This remains true. The question now returns to the depths of God's designs. Is there not "destiny" here? And is not the picture of incomprehensible failure, as we see it in the life of Jesus, the final expression and concentration of a basic attitude within God Himself? With all the reverence and discretion which these questions demand, a man feels himself obliged to say that God really experiences "destiny" in His relations with the world and in a sense that is unique. His nature is such that He can experience this. And this capacity for such experience is His ultimate glory. It is identical with the fact that He loves; or rather, that He *is actually* loving; or, even more fully, that He is "Love." This is the ultimate meaning of sentences like those in John's first epistle: "He that loveth not, knoweth not God, for God is charity"[56] and "God is charity; and he that abideth in charity abideth in God, and God in him" (4:8,16). This is truly a love that "surpasses all knowledge" (Eph. 3:19).

In the course of this discussion the word "destiny" has been transformed. It has now nothing in common with the original meaning we gave it. It has penetrated into the realm of God's holy life and it now denotes something, possible only in God, valid only for God, capable of being understood only from the inner pattern of revelation. But this "destiny" is profoundly tragic. Yet another distinction still has to be made. It is not tragic in the sense analysed earlier, because God knows nothing of the constriction and frustration from which tragedy derives on earth. This is itself the echo of a mystery in God but within a world disturbed through sin. For the tragic element in God there exists no name, and we must rest content with an expression at once simple and yet able to reveal to the man who reflects upon it an ever growing depth, glory, and fruitfulness. It is the earnestness of God's love. Its final expression is Christ's cross. The cross is therefore the absolute symbol. To the man who repudiates it, the world remains self-enclosed and unintelligible.

This knowledge signifies that we have broken through the barrier of human thought, but knowledge becomes Christian in the measure in which it approaches this. If it were attained, it would consume the very heart, but the heart too is Christian to the extent to which it is warmed by its radiance.

---

56. This does not signify that only a man ready to love God can know God, who is eminently Love, but that Love is possible, as John insists, only from God, in that through grace He bestows that attitude which is uniquely His. This becomes in John the recurring circle of Christian existence. He alone knows God who loves God. But only the man to whom God has given it has this love, and this in its turn presupposes that he believes in God, and therefore knows him. All this is that "rebirth from above" of which John also speaks; it is the newness brought by Christ (John 8:23, 47).

This means that the believer must participate in God's "destiny" as
220 Christ declared to His followers: "The disciple is not above the master, nor the servant above his lord. It is enough for the disciple to be as his master and the servant as his lord" (Matt. 10:24–25). This is no easy task. Apart from the opposition and persecution that the believer meets because of his attachment to Christ, there is the other, even more tormenting, problem: to have to be on the side of a person who appears questionable to the world. This is brought out in Paul's grave words about the scandal of the cross (1 Cor. 1:18–25).

This vision is rendered more difficult by the memory that Christians have of the great era of the Middle Ages. For more than a thousand years in the West revelation provided the innermost content of the prevailing culture. The believer involuntarily accepts the existence it portrays as absolutely right, so that anyone who repudiates it has, in his eyes, strayed from the secure and right view of humanity and the world. Ultimately, this judgment is a true one but we must not forget that for a very long time Christians have not had the main direction of human and world affairs. With all its grandeur, the Middle Ages represented one particular pattern, in which the historically active, the spiritual and religious tendencies existed in mutual harmony. Later, the direction of culture gradually moved away from revelation and the real situation, hitherto concealed, was made apparent, namely, that revelation does not derive from the world and that its demands are opposed to man's spontaneous will.

The believer must now assume the burden of existence as we have been describing it. In so doing, he is faced with a twofold danger: the first, that of toning down and secularizing Christ's will in order to conform to the community in which he lives; the second, of taking Christ's will earnestly but lapsing into a mood of pessimism that abandons all control of the world or even into a ghetto mentality, the outlook of a despised minority. Neither trend should be allowed to develop. The Christian ought to respond to his master's call "with his whole heart, his whole soul, and his whole mind" (Matt. 22:37), knowing that this is the "one thing necessary." At the same time he must take his task of directing the world with that earnestness demanded by Christ's will which is the will of the Creator (cf. John 1:3)—and this, despite all the seeming contradictions with which he may meet.

In this process consists man's essential development—the figure of the new man in the new creation, what one day, when it has passed through the fire of judgment, will abide eternally. When this is consciously understood, there is a special term to designate it—a term given by Paul from deep personal experience. Paul calls it hope. We have already quoted the grand passage from the Epistle to the Romans (8:24–25) where this occurs. We conclude these reflections with its closing sentences: "For we are saved by hope. But hope that is seen, is not hope. For what a man seeth, why doth he hope for it? But if we hope for that which we see not; we wait for it with patience."

Designed by Fiona Cecile Clarke, the CLUNY *logo depicts a monk at work in the scriptorium, with a cat sitting at his feet.*

The monk represents our mission to emulate the invaluable contributions of the monks of Cluny in preserving the libraries of the West, our strivings to know and love the truth.

The cat at the monk's feet is Pangur Bán, from the eponymous Irish poem of the 9th century. The anonymous poet compares his scholarly pursuit of truth with the cat's happy hunting of mice. The depiction of Pangur Bán is an homage to the work of the monks of Irish monasteries and a sign of the joy we at Cluny take in our trade.

"Messe ocus Pangur Bán,
cechtar nathar fria saindan:
bíth a menmasam fri seilgg,
mu memna céin im saincheirdd."

Made in the USA
Middletown, DE
18 February 2025

71229099R00129